T0136461

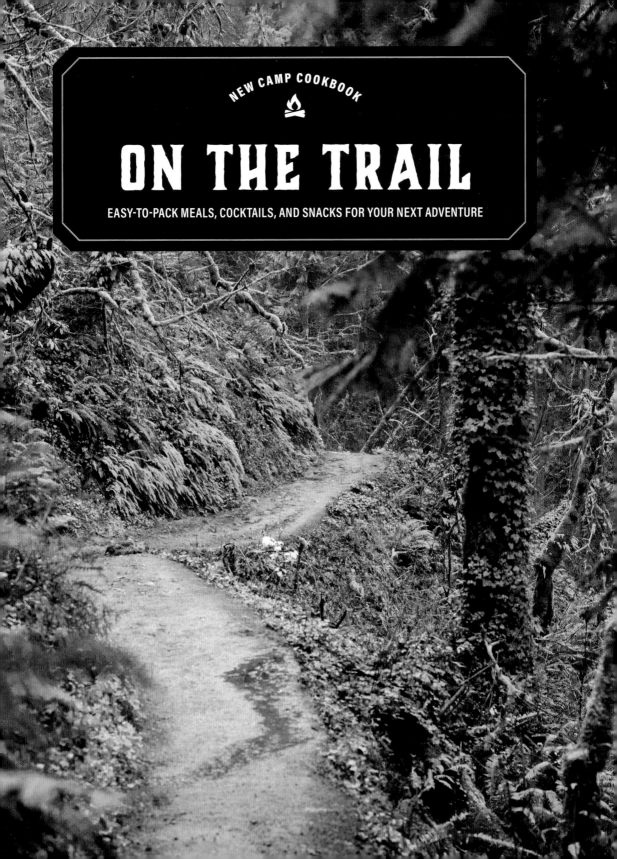

NEW CAMP COOKBOOK

ON THE TRAIL

EASY-TO-PACK MEALS, COCKTAILS, AND SNACKS FOR YOUR NEXT ADVENTURE

Quarto.com

© 2024 Quarto Publishing Group USA Inc.
Text © 2024 Emily Vikre
Photography © 2024 Hanna Voxland

First Published in 2024 by The Harvard Common Press, an imprint of The Quarto Group, 100 Cummings Center, Suite 265-D, Beverly, MA 01915, USA.
T (978) 282-9590 F (978) 283-2742

The Harvard Common Press titles are also available at discount for retail, wholesale, promotional, and bulk purchase. For details, contact the Special Sales Manager by email at specialsales@quarto.com or by mail at The Quarto Group, Attn: Special Sales Manager, 100 Cummings Center, Suite 265-D, Beverly, MA 01915, USA.

28 27 26 25 24   1 2 3 4 5

ISBN: 978-0-7603-8508-1

Digital edition published in 2024
eISBN: 978-0-7603-8509-8

The recipes beginning on pages 59, 60, 63, 118, 120 and the text on pages 40–41 and 55–56 have been adapted from *Camp Cocktails* (Harvard Common Press, 2020). The recipes beginning on pages 15, 16, 23, 30, 71, 72, 75, 104 and the text on page 34 have been adapted from *The Family Camp Cookboo*k (Harvard Common Press, 2022).

Library of Congress Cataloging-in-Publication Data available

Interior Design: The Sly Studio
Cover Images: Hanna Voxland
Page Layout: Megan Jones Design
Photography: Emily Vikre on pages 6, 8, 10, 17, 21, 25, 28, 32, 45, 65, 66, 77, 78, 80, 105, 116, 122, 130, 133, and 144; Hanna Voxland on pages 1, 7, 14, 18, 24, 26, 27, 31, 34, 38, 41, 42, 46, 48, 50, 54, 56, 58, 61, 62, 70, 73, 84, 87, 88, 91, 92, 95, 96, 99, 104, 106, 109, 110, 119, 121, 134, 137, 139, and 140; Shutterstock on pages 49, 74, 100, 126, and 129
Illustration: Shutterstock

Printed in China

NEW CAMP COOKBOOK

ON THE TRAIL

EASY-TO-PACK MEALS, COCKTAILS, AND SNACKS FOR YOUR NEXT ADVENTURE

EMILY VIKRE

HARVARD
COMMON
PRESS

CONTENTS

CHAPTER 1
PACKABLE SNACKABLES

CHAPTER 2
PREPPED MEALS

CHAPTER 3
FLASK COCKTAILS

CHAPTER 4
EASY TO ASSEMBLE

INTRODUCTION

When I think back through my memories of backpacking and canoeing trips, of being on trail for a few days or more at a time, food is often memorable for all the wrong reasons: It ran out, or we weren't able to cook it because it was raining too hard to even start a camp stove, or it froze solid in a snowbank. (Partially reheated, partially frozen chili is not the stuff of which culinary dreams are made.)

But here's the thing: Being on trail is about spending a lot of time outdoors and away from it all. With the constraints placed on you by having to carry every piece of camping equipment, cooking equipment, and food supplies via your own person-power, food can become a logistical problem to solve more than something to enjoy. At the same time, when you are active and constantly outside for days in a row, you get so hungry that fussiness in eating evaporates, replaced by gratitude for a full belly—and the renewed energy it provides.

Now, some people take food as fuel to the extreme. My husband's ex is a very serious camper and survivalist. She makes her own beef jerky and she *doesn't even season it*. Yikes. Backpacking is a sanctified and invigorating form of suffering, but there is no need to suffer that much.

And here's my take: If one area becomes a little less suffer-y, that gives you greater bandwidth to suffer in another. Pack lighter, hurt less from the weight of your pack. Hurt more from going farther instead. You get the idea. So, even though there's basically nothing that I can do to save you from the texture of backpacking food, I can at least make sure your jerky is beautifully seasoned so that chewing it is a treat, not a chore, leaving more energy for summitting that next peak.

This book explores just a small portion of what you can cook within the crucible of the limitations of trail food—that is to say, with ingredients that are shelf stable, lightweight, and extremely fast cooking (or no cook). I'm not trying to revolutionize what trail food is, but this book offers a variety of fun ideas for combining traditional backpacking food in new ways. First, there are recipes for snacks, meals, and drinks you can prep at home to pack with you. Second, there are recipes for fast and easy but still flavorful camping meals to make on trail with a few options for each meal of the day—breakfast, lunch/snack, dinner, and even some sweet treats. And third, there are recipes to get you started with dehydrating your ingredients and snacks if that is something you'd like to try.

TRAIL WISDOM

As I alluded to earlier, the dirty little secret—or, perhaps more accurately, the amazingly helpful truth—of trail food is that when you are outside and on the move all day, *all* food tastes amazing. Which is good, because even the most gourmet of trail food has to be simple and streamlined. What are the main things that make for good trail food?

1. **Shelf stable.** When you're eating on the trail, you're going to be away from sources of refrigeration (unless you are winter camping, which brings its own set of considerations) and you will likely be carrying your food with you in a backpack. So, be sure the food you pack is shelf stable. Some foods that we usually refrigerate but that are actually preserved foods, such as salami, summer sausage, or hard cheese, can be carried safely for several days.

2. **Lightweight.** If you're lugging your food with you—whether on your back or in a boat—you are going to want to be conscientious about how much it weighs. Now, I have never been, and never will be, an ultralight backpacker or thru-hiker, so I've never thought about weight in the obsessive way that those exploits require. But, when you're carrying all your things on your back, you're going to be keenly aware of how heavy it is. Don't let your food weigh you down. Choose lightweight options, including dehydrated foods.

3. **Easy to prepare.** Some more things that weigh a lot? Fuel and cookware. By choosing meals that can be cooked quickly and using a minimum of dishes, you can simplify your life at mealtimes and lighten your load.

4. **Nutritionally balanced.** When you're on the go in the fresh air, you use up a lot of energy. You want to make sure you plan meals that include all the major nutrients—fats, proteins, and carbohydrates—as well as micronutrient-rich foods with ingredients like vegetables, fruits, and nuts.

5. **Varied.** Some people do fine eating the same thing day after day. But for me, variety is essential if I don't want to slowly lose my mind. I love dehydrated cheesy rice to a weird degree, but if I eat it for more than two dinners in a row, I will wave a white flag and straight up quit rather than eat it one more time. Using a variety of starches, switching up your spices, and incorporating different dehydrated vegetables or dried fruits are all great ways of making sure your meals taste varied and complex. Even if they are mostly minute rice.

Also, meal planning is imperative! You'll want to figure out how many calories you need per day, which will depend on you, your metabolism, and how strenuous your outdoor adventures are. Then map out your meals for each day (breakfast, quick lunch, adequate snacks, dinner) and pack the ingredients for each meal together in a lightweight, sealable container. Make sure you also bring a couple of extra meals. It adds extra weight, but it is best to be prepared! Make sure to have water sources planned as well as having a proper water sanitation and filtration system.

I am not a gearhead, so I don't have strong opinions about camping gear, and that includes cooking gear. Just make sure you have a lightweight stove, a cooking pot (which you may find you eat directly out of for a lot of meals), a camping knife, utensils (you can't go wrong with a camping spork!), a camp cup, and dishes, if you want them. You may also need to have a bear canister or bear bag for hanging your food in a tree, depending on where you are camping.

So make sure your hiking boots are broken in, your olive oil is packed in a lightweight, well-sealed container, and your route is planned. Let's hit the trails.

CHAPTER ONE

PACKABLE SNACKABLES

A good half of what you're likely eating on trail is snacks. They pad out your meals, double as dessert, and keep you going throughout the day while you are eating up the miles. As such an important part of your trail food arsenal, you'll want to make sure they are as delectable as they are necessary!

APRICOT CHERRY SNACK BALLS

MAKES 16-18 BALLS

I've been told these little fruit and nut bites are "addictively delicious." They're a bit like fruit and nut energy bars, except round, which is obviously more fun because it's kind of like edible polka dots.

INGREDIENTS

1 cup (130 g) dried apricots

1 cup (120 g) dried cherries

1 cup (123 g) toasted, shelled pistachios

1 tablespoon (20 g) honey

1 teaspoon lemon zest

½ cup (42 g) toasted, shredded coconut (or sesame seeds), for rolling

MAKE IT

1. Combine the apricots, cherries, pistachios, honey, and lemon zest in a food processor. Pulse/run the processor until everything is very finely chopped together but not turned into a paste—it takes a minute or so.

2. Line a baking sheet with parchment paper and put the coconut (or sesame seeds) in a small bowl. Roll a tablespoonful (6 g) of the mixture at a time into balls and roll the balls in the coconut (or sesame seeds) to coat, then place them on the baking sheet. Put the finished balls into the fridge to firm up for 1 hour.

3. After they have chilled, they can be stored and transported in an airtight container for up to a week. Put parchment paper between layers to prevent sticking.

GRANOLA BARS

MAKES 10 BARS

Making your own granola bars may seem like overkill, something you only do if you also live on a homestead and wear bonnets and raise chickens and make your own butter. All of which, actually, are activities that I'm totally here for, so maybe that explains something. Anyway, if you ever look at your grocery receipts and notice just how much money you spend on organic granola bars for your three-year-old who consumes them like they are the base of the food pyramid, suddenly making your own granola bars seems like a reasonable and frugal activity. Plus they taste better than the store-bought kind, and they pack quite well. Throw a container in your backpack to prevent midhike meltdowns.

INGREDIENTS

1¼ cups (125 g) rolled oats

⅓ cup (46 g) whole wheat flour (replace with ground flaxseed for a gluten-free bar)

3 tablespoons (27 g) cornmeal

1 cup (175 g) finely chopped pitted dates

1 teaspoon salt

½ teaspoon ground cinnamon

⅓ cup (115 g) honey

¼ cup (60 ml) olive oil

¼ cup (65 g) creamy peanut butter

½ teaspoon lemon zest

MAKE IT

1. Preheat the oven to 350°F (180°C, or gas mark 4). Line an 8" × 8" (20 × 20 cm) baking pan with parchment paper. (Aluminum foil will also work. With most baking projects I don't use parchment paper, but for these I really recommend lining your baking pan if you want the bars to come out without breaking apart.)

2. In one bowl, combine the oats, whole wheat flour, cornmeal, dates, salt, and cinnamon. In a separate bowl, whisk together the honey, olive oil, peanut butter, and lemon zest. Scrape the wet ingredients into the bowl of the dry ingredients and stir well until everything is completely coated.

3. Dump the mixture into the prepared pan and pat it into an even layer with your fingers (there's enough olive oil that it won't stick to your fingers). Bake for 20 to 25 minutes or until well browned around the edges but still soft in the center. Cool the bars to room temperature, then use a sharp knife to cut into 10 pieces, about 4" × 1½" (10 × 4 cm). Stack the bars in a sealed, airtight container with parchment paper between the layers and allow them to chill in the fridge for at least another 30 minutes to fully set them. Store and transport in the airtight container.

TIP

Can't do nuts? Tahini or sunflower seed butter will also work well in these granola bars.

GRAIN-FREE BLUEBERRY BREAKFAST BARS

MAKES 9 BARS

I have to start by saying this is not really my recipe. I am, in fact, allergic to almonds and several other nuts. My dad, on the other hand, is gluten and dairy free (as opposed to me, the gluten and dairy fiend!). When he first had to change his diet based on this discovery, I went on something of a grain-free baking spree to find fun treats for him, even though I couldn't eat most of them. These are adapted from a blog I found called *The Defined Dish*. The use of almond butter and coconut flour (which behaves *completely* differently from any other type of flour, so don't try to substitute) makes these hearty, chewy, and packed with protein and healthy fats for a quick start to the day or to eat while on the trail. And I will never know what they taste like. *C'est la vie!*

INGREDIENTS

1 cup (240 g) almond butter

2 large eggs

¼ cup (80 g) maple syrup

1 tablespoon (14 g) coconut oil, melted

½ teaspoon vanilla extract

Zest of 1 large lemon

1 tablespoon (8 g) coconut flour

½ teaspoon baking soda

½ teaspoon salt

½ cup (85 g) dried blueberries

MAKE IT

1. Preheat the oven to 350°F (180°C, or gas mark 4). Grease an 8" × 8" (20 × 20 cm) baking dish with coconut oil and line it with parchment paper.

2. In a large bowl, combine the almond butter, eggs, maple syrup, coconut oil, vanilla extract, and lemon zest. Using a handheld mixer, whisk together until smooth. Add the remaining ingredients and mix until combined.

3. Spread the batter into the prepared pan and bake until cooked through, about 25 minutes. A toothpick pricked into the middle of the bars should come out clean. Allow to cool in the pan for 10 to 15 minutes, then cut into squares and transfer to a wire rack to cool completely. Once cool, wrap individually in plastic wrap or foil. Store in the fridge or freezer until ready to pack.

TIP

You should also be able to make these with cashew butter instead of almond butter.

TOASTER PASTRIES

MAKES 9 PASTRIES

I once read an article in *Outside* magazine by an avid thru-hiker who had swapped his instant oatmeal for cold cinnamon toaster pastries to allow him to get going even faster in the morning, and he swore by the change. I can't really get behind cold commercial toaster pastries. Their overlap with cardboard is too strong. But cold *homemade* toaster pastries—that's another story.

If I think about it, I don't really expect you to make homemade toaster pastries—which are a bit of a fuss, to be honest—to wrap and bring camping. But isn't it great to know you can? And this way if you decide to go the distance and make them, you get buttery, tender pastry around the start-your-engine-fast sugar-cinnamon filling. This recipe is adapted from one developed originally by the lovely bakers at King Arthur Flour. And *psst*—I'm going to let you in on a little secret: If you want to skip making the crust from scratch, use two store-bought pie crusts rolled out instead, which will work beautifully and be substantially simpler. But if you want the whole project, here you go!

INGREDIENTS

FOR THE PASTRY

2 cups (256 g) all-purpose flour

1 tablespoon (13 g) granulated sugar

1 teaspoon salt

1 cup (2 sticks or 225 g) very cold salted butter, cut into small cubes

1 large egg, at refrigerator temperature

2 tablespoons (30 ml) milk, at refrigerator temperature

FOR THE FILLING

½ cup (112 g) packed dark brown sugar

1 teaspoon ground cinnamon

4 teaspoons all-purpose flour

1 large egg, whisked (to use to seal the pastry before baking)

MAKE IT

1. To make the dough, combine the flour, sugar, and salt in a large bowl. Using your fingers, pinch in the cold butter, rubbing it gently and quickly into the dough until you have a mixture with pea-size lumps.

2. Whisk together the egg and milk. Make a well in the center of the flour mixture and pour the milk-egg mixture into it. Stir until everything is cohesive, and knead a couple of times just until it comes together into a ball.

3. To prepare the tarts, divide the dough in half and use your hands to pat and shape each half into a thick rectangle that's about 3" × 5" (8 × 13 cm). Wrap it in plastic wrap and refrigerate for at least half an hour to allow the gluten to relax and the dough to chill. (You can leave refrigerated for up to 2 days, but if you chill for longer than a half hour, let it sit on the counter at room temperature for about 20 minutes before attempting to roll it out.)

4. Make the filling by stirring together all the filling ingredients except the egg.

(continued)

5. To assemble the tarts, place one of the dough rectangles on a floured surface and roll into a rectangle that is 9" × 12" (23 × 30 cm). Trim the edges to make a perfect rectangle and then cut into thirds length- and height-wise to form nine 3" × 4" (8 × 10 cm) rectangles. Repeat with the second dough rectangle.

6. Brush the whisked "filling" egg over the entire surface of half of the small rectangles. Then, spoon a heaping tablespoon of filling into the center of each, leaving at least ½ inch (1 cm) around the border. Place a second dough rectangle on top of each filling-topped rectangle, then use a fork to firmly press around the edges of each rectangle pocket to seal the sides together. Prick the top of each pop tart with a fork to make small holes to allow steam to escape.

7. Place the tarts on a parchment paper–lined baking sheet and put them in the fridge for 30 minutes. This will prevent the butter from completely melting and leaking out as they bake. Meanwhile, preheat the oven to 350°F (180°C, or gas mark 4).

8. After the 30 minutes of chilling, transfer the baking sheet to the oven and bake the tarts until they are golden brown, about 20 to 25 minutes. Remove from the oven and allow to fully cool on the tray. (We are not going to be icing these because we are pretending they make a reasonable breakfast, you sugar fiend!) Once they are cooled, you can wrap them individually or put them in a rigid container for transporting.

TIP

The thing that makes these so much better than commercial Pop-Tarts is the tender pastry, but this does also make them more breakable. So wrap them well. I think they taste even better when they are a day or two old, but I wouldn't recommend taking them on a trip that is longer than a weekend.

CHERRY-PECAN GRANOLA

MAKES ABOUT 6 SERVINGS

Most of my history with granola has precisely nothing to do with camping, but humor me anyway. From age twelve to age twenty, I ate granola with yogurt for breakfast every. single. day. Yes, there were exceptions for holidays and travel, but the point is, I ate a lot of granola. I had strong opinions about granola: big clusters, no nuts, dried fruit, lightly spiced. In fact, I was fond enough of granola that during freshman year of college, my roommate and I stole one of the bulk serving bins of granola from the cafeteria so we could have a source of granola that was not closed in the middle of the night. (Hopefully, it's been long enough that the statute of limitations is up on that little moment of delinquency from an otherwise resolute rule-follower.) Then, I developed an oat allergy.

So, I don't actually eat granola anymore (sigh). But my family does. This recipe is tailored to my husband's granola preferences, and we know he has good taste, because he married me. Make a batch of this granola at home and pack it in a jar or sealed container to bring with you to camp. You can serve it with powdered milk or freeze-dried yogurt drops for breakfast, but it's also excellent sprinkled over cooked fruit for a dessert (see the Sautéed Apples on page 104 or Wild Berry Crumble on page 111).

INGREDIENTS

2 cups (180 g) rolled oats

1½ cups (150 g) roughly chopped raw pecans

½ teaspoon ground cinnamon

¼ teaspoon ground nutmeg

¼ teaspoon sea salt

¾ cup (241 g) maple syrup

3 tablespoons (45 ml) olive oil

1 teaspoon vanilla extract

1½ cups (180 g) dried cherries

MAKE IT

1. Preheat the oven to 250°F (120°C, or gas mark ½).

2. In a large bowl, combine the oats, pecans, spices, and salt. Pour the maple syrup, oil, and vanilla extract over and toss well to coat—the best tool for mixing is your hands, even though you'll get stupendously sticky.

3. Spread out the mixture in a single layer on a rimmed baking sheet (it's helpful to line the baking sheet with parchment paper, but it's not necessary). Bake in the oven for 45 to 50 minutes, then remove from the oven and use a large spatula to flip the granola over in large pieces, trying to break it apart as little as possible. (Don't worry about some breakage, which is inevitable. You're just trying to minimize it so you can have bigger clusters at the end.) Return the granola to the oven and bake for another 45 to 50 minutes or until it is completely dry and no longer chewy if you take a bite.

(continued)

4. Remove from the oven and allow to cool completely. Then break into the size of clusters that you like best, mix with the dried cherries, and store in a sealed container for up to 2 weeks.

5. To serve, in your camp bowl combine your desired amount of powdered milk or freeze-dried yogurt with some water to make liquid, and stir well. Add a scoop of granola.

CAMPER'S COOKIES

MAKES 2 DOZEN

These are a classic take on cowboy cookies from my favorite camping-savvy neighbors. We were only allowed cookies at Christmastime growing up, so seeing people use cookies as a granola bar stand-in was a life-altering, joy-inducing discovery indeed. These cookies are sturdy for packing, buttery for eating, and contain every snacky niblet you could possibly want.

INGREDIENTS

2⅓ cups (292 g) all-purpose flour

1 teaspoon baking soda

1 teaspoon ground cinnamon

¾ teaspoon salt

2 cups (180 g) rolled oats (old-fashioned oats, not quick cooking)

½ cup (42 g) shredded coconut

½ cup (50 g) roughly chopped pecans

1 cup (145 g) raisins

1 cup (203 g) candy-coated chocolate pieces (like M&Ms)

1 cup (224 g) unsalted butter, softened to room temperature

1½ cups (360 g) light brown sugar

½ cup (100 g) granulated sugar

2 large eggs and 1 egg yolk, at room temperature

1 teaspoon vanilla extract

MAKE IT

1. Preheat the oven to 350°F (180°C, or gas mark 4). In a large bowl, combine all the dry ingredients—flour, baking soda, cinnamon, salt, oats, coconut, pecans, raisins, and chocolate pieces—and stir together to combine.

2. In the bowl of a stand mixer fitted with a paddle attachment, blend together the butter and sugars until fluffy (you can also use a handheld mixer). Add the eggs and yolk 1 at a time, followed by the vanilla, continuing to beat on a medium-low speed until well combined and smooth.

3. Fold the dry ingredients into the wet ingredients using a rubber spatula or wooden spoon, mixing until just combined.

4. Scoop 2-inch (5 cm) balls of dough onto baking sheets (line the baking sheets with parchment paper for easier cleanup, if you'd like), leaving about 2 inches (5 cm) between each cookie for room to spread. Refrigerate the dough balls for about 20 minutes before baking. (This is not absolutely required but definitely recommended.)

5. Bake 1 sheet at a time until the edges of the cookies are brown and set but the centers of the cookies are still just a bit soft, about 12 to 14 minutes. Allow the cookies to set by cooling them on the sheets for a few minutes before transferring them to a wire rack to cool completely. These cookies store well in an airtight container and can be packed into a zip-top plastic bag for hikes and outings.

TRAIL MIX #1:
A TWIST ON TRADITIONAL

MAKES 3 CUPS (450 G)

There's a reason GORP stands for "good old raisins and peanuts." The combination is classic, timeless, and tasty. BUT it's even better with pecans. When pecans are toasted, they are a most superior nut, roasted and sweet and complex. Because they are kind of a fancy nut, I stretch them here by adding some other bulky nut of your choice. Other than that, this trail mix hews pretty close to the traditional, aside from combining raisins with dried cranberries for an extra sweet-tart pop.

INGREDIENTS

1 cup (100 g) raw pecans

½ cup (65 g) raw almonds
(or other nut)

1 tablespoon (15 ml) olive oil

Pinch of sea salt

½ cup (60 g) dried cranberries

½ cup (80 g) golden raisins

½ cup (87 g) dark chocolate chips

MAKE IT

1. Preheat the oven to 300°F (150°C, or gas mark 2). Toss the pecans and almonds with the olive oil and a hefty pinch of sea salt and spread onto a baking sheet. Bake in the oven, stirring occasionally, until toasted but not deep brown, approximately 10 minutes. Allow to completely cool to room temperature.

2. Mix the nuts, dried fruit, and chocolate chips together in a large bowl, and then divide into sealable bags.

TIP

Change it up: If you're a fan of the cashew-Craisin mixes that are popular in the grocery snack aisle these days, you can take a cue from them. Use cashews instead of pecans and white chocolate chips instead of dark chocolate.

TRAIL MIX #2: KINDA FANCY

MAKES 6 CUPS (1015 G)

Yes, this is a snack mix we serve at our bar at Vikre Distillery. But my husband often grabs some to snack on, and it winds up in his car, and our kids spot it and love it. So, it's a favorite for the whole family and makes a fun trail mix alternative. Fiery crunchy wasabi peas, savory sesame sticks, and bits of nori take cheesy Goldfish in an unexpectedly tasty direction.

INGREDIENTS

4 cups (804 g) cheesy Goldfish crackers (you could use other cheese crackers, but then you wouldn't get to think about how funny it is to have fish and seaweed together in your snack mix)

1 cup (120 g) sesame sticks

1 cup (91 g) wasabi peas

1 sheet nori, cut into short, thin strips, kind of like seaweed confetti

MAKE IT

Stir all of the ingredients together and transfer them into a tightly sealed container—that's it!

TRAIL MIX #3:
THE CHUNKY MONKEY

MAKES 6 CUPS (1015 G)

Speaking of my husband's car, apparently it's the place where all the snacks in our family live. There is also an ever-present jar of peanut butter pretzels in there. They make a great emergency snack when hunger has tipped over the thin edge from vaguely uncomfortable to anger inducing. And that save-the-day quality gave me the idea to include them in a trail mix. The peanut butter had me thinking of peanut butter and banana sandwiches, so in went banana chips. And at that point, the addition of dark chocolate was a no-brainer.

INGREDIENTS

1 cup (100 g) halved walnuts

½ tablespoon (8 ml) olive oil

Pinch of sea salt

3 cups (100 g) peanut butter-filled pretzels

1 cup (175 g) dark chocolate chips or chocolate chunks

1 cup (127 g) dried banana chips

MAKE IT

1. Preheat the oven to 300°F (150°C, or gas mark 2). Toss the walnuts with olive oil and a pinch of sea salt and spread on a baking sheet. Bake until toasted and fragrant, about 10 minutes. Allow to completely cool to room temperature.

2. Mix all the ingredients in a large bowl, and then divide into sealable bags.

TRAIL MIX #4: TROPICAL TREAT

MAKES 3½ CUPS (600 G)

The last thing you want when you are on the trail for a long time is to have only one type of trail mix. It starts as an enticing snack, a reward for a trail well trekked, but by day three or four, you find yourself having to choke it down. By the time you're done with your trip you swear you will never look at a peanut or raisin again. Which is precisely why I'm including so many recipes for trail mix here, to make sure you take the cue to change things up! This particular trail mix is a playful, tropical variation on the fruit and nut theme.

INGREDIENTS

½ cup (42 g) coconut flakes
(these are wider coconut pieces
than shredded coconut)

1 cup (150 g) shelled pistachios

1 cup (130 g) cashews

1 tablespoon (14 g) coconut oil

Pinch of sea salt

½ cup (65 g) dried apricots,
cut into quarters

½ cup (64 g) dried kiwi slices,
cut into quarters

MAKE IT

1. Preheat the oven to 300°F (150°C, or gas mark 2). Spread the coconut flakes on a baking sheet and bake until lightly browned, about 6 minutes. Remove from the oven and transfer to a large bowl to cool.

2. Toss the pistachios and cashews with coconut oil and a pinch of sea salt. Spread them on the baking sheet and bake in the oven, stirring occasionally, until toasted, about 10 minutes. Remove from the oven and allow to cool completely.

3. In the large bowl, mix together the coconut, nuts, and dried fruit pieces until fully combined. Divide into sealable bags.

CHOOSE YOUR OWN ADVENTURE TRAIL MIX

There's nothing wrong with GORP, the most classic trail mix. In fact, I used to practically live off it on camping trips. Or to be more accurate, I lived off the M&Ms I meticulously picked out of it. But, when it comes down to it, trail mix is really just a mix of things you like to snack on, all thrown together. So why not choose your own adventure? Choose a nut (if you can have nuts), a dried fruit or two, a treat, and a crunchy element, and build the trail mix of your dreams. Here are some options to get you started.

Nutty Option

Peanuts

Toasted almonds

Walnuts

Toasted hazelnuts

Pepitas

Fruity Option

Dried cherries

Dried mango bits and golden raisins

Dried cranberries

Banana chips

Chopped dried figs

Dried apricots

Sweet Option

Chocolate chips

M&Ms

White chocolate chips

Yogurt-covered raisins

Milk chocolate chips or disks

Chopped crystalized ginger

Crunchy Option

Pretzels

Toasted coconut flakes

Popcorn

Toasted oat Os cereal (such as Cheerios)

Rye pretzels

Sesame sticks

Chex cereal

CHAPTER TWO

PREPPED MEALS

A huge variety of prepacked, ready-to-rehydrate camping meals are available these days, which are an amazing asset to have when you are planning a trip. But it can also be fun to prep some of your own meal mixes. This gives you total control over what's in your food and how it is seasoned.

SPICE MIX #1:
MIDDLE EASTERN INSPIRED

MAKES JUST UNDER ¼ CUP (21 G)

One of the best ways to avoid food boredom when on trail is having different herbs and spices available to bring life to your meals. Rice with beans and chili spices is a solidly different eating experience from rice with beans and tagine-inspired spices, just like a solid blue flannel shirt is a *totally different* fashion statement from a buffalo-check flannel shirt. Variations on a theme make the world go around, whether sartorial or spice. Here are a few spice blends to make and bring with you to add variety and pizzazz to your days.

Inspired by the Middle Eastern spice blend *ras el hanout*, I use this combination of spices ad nauseum. It's just so good. It's a perfect balance of sweet, spicy, earthy, warm, and vibrant. Add it to rice or couscous dishes, vegetables, or any meat. It's especially good in dishes with dried fruits and nuts (ahem, so much of camping food!).

INGREDIENTS

1 tablespoon (7 g) ground cumin

½ tablespoon (3 g) ground coriander

1 tablespoon (7 g) paprika

1 teaspoon black pepper

1 teaspoon ground cinnamon

MAKE IT

Mix all ingredients together. Store in an airtight container.

SPICE MIX #2:
GARDEN HERB BLEND

MAKES ABOUT ½ CUP (28 G)

This is a mixture of garden herbs that is incredibly versatile for anything that could use a lift. Dried herbs can never live up to the *oomph* of their fresh counterparts, but they still add a touch of pleasant lightness to a dish.

INGREDIENTS

3 tablespoons (5 g) dried parsley

2 tablespoons (10 g) dried onion flakes

1 tablespoon (9 g) garlic powder

1 tablespoon (3 g) dried dill

½ tablespoon (1 g) dried chives

MAKE IT

Mix all the ingredients together. Store in an airtight container.

SPICE MIX #3:
SOUTHWEST SEASONING

MAKES ABOUT ½ CUP (41 G)

Chili, tacos, quesadillas, breakfast burritos, any Southwestern-inspired food can use a sprinkling of this blend of chili, spices, and oregano.

INGREDIENTS

2 tablespoons (15 g) chili powder

1 tablespoon (7 g) sweet paprika

1 tablespoon (9 g) garlic powder

½ tablespoon ground coriander

½ tablespoon ground cumin

1 teaspoon dried oregano

½ teaspoon cayenne pepper

MAKE IT

Mix all ingredients together. Store in an airtight container.

FORAGED AND FOUND

While I would never recommend planning to rely on wild food when you are camping (how many canoe trips have been ruined by planning to subsist on fresh-caught fish, only to have your hook come up persistently empty!), it can be a fun addition to your trail meals, if you know what you are doing. Foraging, when it comes down to it, is simply going and getting yourself something to eat. Doing that from a supermarket rather than from the field or forest is actually a newfangled trend. I have been foraging since I was a child, brought up to seek out wild berries, pick wild onions, nibble on wood sorrel, and suck on sumac berries as a treat.

Before you start to forage for ingredients from the forest or your backyard, make sure you know what you are doing. Nature isn't joking around. She is abundant and generous, but she can also kill you. Never eat anything if you aren't 100 percent certain that it is safe. In fact, I am an anxious forager—which I think is the best type of forager—and so I only pick and eat foods that I am 150 percent sure are safe. Do not go picking wild foods until you have learned to forage properly. And start by focusing on wild foods that have a wide range, are easy to identify, and don't really have poisonous look-alikes.

The best way to learn to forage is in person, from an expert. Many areas have groups that you can join, with certified herbalists and certified foragers to teach you. Working alongside such people, you can learn to safely identify wild plants by getting to know the multiple characteristics to look for. Always use several points of identification to ensure you know what a plant is, including the habitat, visual cues from different parts of the plant (what its stem, leaves, flowers, and more look like), feel (rough, hairy, smooth, or papery types of characteristics), and smell. Learn the time of year plants grow and companion plants they often grow near, and make sure you carefully learn about any poisonous plants in your area so that you are acutely aware of those as well. Supplement what you learn in person by getting a good field guide to plants in your area. As you learn to forage, you will also learn to protect the plants and ecosystems they live in. To protect rare or endangered species and fragile ecosystems, focus your foraging on plants that are abundant and robust—that is to say, weeds. You can even forage for invasive species. Never pick more than you need. And make

sure you know whether you are even allowed to forage in the area where you are. Remember that picking wild plants from national parks is actually illegal.

Those are a lot of cautions, I know. But once you've done the work, learned what you need to learn, and feel confident enjoying wild berries, mushrooms, and herbs, the results will be worth it.

JUST-ADD-WATER PANCAKES

MAKES ENOUGH MIX FOR ABOUT 40 PANCAKES

If there's one thing other than trail mix that I associate deeply with camping, it's pancake mix. While sometimes it feels like too much trouble or a waste of fuel to cook up a hot breakfast, some days you simply can't get going without it. And pancake mix is the perfect thing for those days. This mixture is easy to batch at home and stores for months. Portion out and pack just the amount you need for your trip, and when a chilly morning rolls around, all you have to do is add water and fry!

INGREDIENTS

4½ cups (563 g) all-purpose flour

¾ cup (90 g) dry powdered milk

⅓ cup (67 g) granulated sugar

2 tablespoons (30 g) baking powder

1½ teaspoons (9 g) salt

1 teaspoon baking soda

½ cup (80 g) small dried fruit such as dried blueberries or currants (optional)

Butter or cooking oil for frying

Maple sugar or maple syrup for serving (optional)

MAKE IT

1. To make the mix, combine all the ingredients except the butter/oil and whisk until fully mixed. Store in an airtight container for up to 6 months.

2. When ready to use, measure out the desired amount of mix into a mixing bowl: 1 cup of pancake mix makes about 4 to 5 pancakes. For every 1 cup of pancake mix, whisk in ¾ cup water, until just combined. (It will still be slightly lumpy. Don't overmix.)

3. Heat a cooking pan or griddle over your burner over medium heat and add butter or cooking oil to coat the pan. Scoop scant ¼ cup scoops of the batter into the pan. Fry until bubbles appear and the edges look browned, about 2 minutes. Flip the pancakes and cook on the other sides until golden brown. Repeat with the remaining batter until all the pancakes are cooked, using more butter or oil to grease the pan between each batch. Serve plain or top with a bit of maple sugar or syrup.

MINESTRONE SOUP MIX

MAKES 1 SERVING

Even though a wide variety of great prepackaged camping meals are now available, it can also be fun to make your own. If you have dehydrated vegetables and beans, you can take matters into your own hands when it comes to preparing rehydratable meals. Minestrone, a simple mixture of noodles, beans, and veggies of your choice, is a great place to start!

You can make your own dehydrated ingredients (see the dehydrator bits and bobs section on page 127), but there are a variety of sources online as well.

INGREDIENTS

½ cup (about 31 g) mixed dehydrated vegetables, preferably carrots, zucchini, and corn or broccoli

2 tablespoons dehydrated tomatoes

½ teaspoon Spice Mix #2 (page 39)

1 cube vegetable bouillon

⅓ cup (40 g) dehydrated white beans (not uncooked white beans, but camper's beans that have been cooked and then dehydrated)

¼ cup (75 g) macaroni noodles

Salt to taste

MAKE IT

1. Combine all the ingredients in a sealable plastic bag.

2. When ready to prepare, combine your soup mix with 2 cups of water and bring to a boil. Simmer for 8 minutes, until the noodles are tender and the beans have rehydrated. Season with additional salt if needed (this will depend on your bouillon).

TIP

Finding freeze-dried/dehydrated ingredients: Some specialty grocery stores carry an assortment of dried produce in their bulk section, but more often you'll want to buy these types of ingredients from companies whose focus is making camping food ingredients. There are a number of them that you can find online. Here are a few:

- Harmony House Foods

- AlpineAire Foods from REI

- Karen's Naturals

- Mother Earth Products

"FRIED" RICE MIX

SERVES 2

This dish doesn't really fit the traditional idea of fried rice. It's more of a rice bowl or medley. But I think of it as fried rice because you fry the rice before adding water. Chopped dried mango adds surprising sweet-tart punchiness to the umami-rich rice and beef jerky. If you've packed some sturdy fresh vegetables with you, like sugar snap peas or green onions, these can be nice to slice up and stir in as well.

INGREDIENTS

1 cup (195 g) instant rice

2 ounces (55 g) beef jerky, chopped into small pieces

¼ cup (30 g) chopped dried mango

¼ cup (12 g) dehydrated peas

½ teaspoon ground ginger

½ teaspoon garlic powder

1 teaspoon brown sugar

2 tablespoons (30 ml) olive oil (or sesame oil)

2 tablespoons (30 ml) soy sauce in packets

1 tablespoon (15 ml) vinegar (preferably rice vinegar)

Salt to taste

MAKE IT

1. Combine the rice, beef jerky, mango, peas, ginger, garlic powder, and brown sugar in a sealable bag.

2. To prepare, add the oil to a pot, then add the rice mixture. Cook, stirring constantly over medium heat until the rice starts to toast, just a minute or so.

3. Add 1¼ cups (300 ml) water plus 1 tablespoon (15 ml) of the soy sauce and bring to a boil, continuing to stir. Remove from the heat, cover, and allow to stand for 10 minutes, until the water is absorbed and the rice mixture is rehydrated. Add additional soy sauce, vinegar, and salt to taste.

TIP

Want to make it a little more like a traditional fried rice with egg bits? Simply scramble a serving of eggs from egg crystals/ dehydrated eggs following the packaged directions before you start the rice dish. Set it aside while you cook the rice, and stir it in when you are ready to serve.

COUSCOUS MIX WITH OLIVES, NUTS, AND DRIED FRUIT

SERVES 2

Couscous is a brilliant trail food. On the Venn diagram of starches it is right in the overlap between pasta and rice—rice texture, pasta flavor! And it cooks in minutes with the addition of boiling water. You can use it as a starchy base for nearly any combination of spices, protein, and other ingredients, but its North African origins make it an especially good fit for flavors inspired by that region.

INGREDIENTS

½ cup (83 g) couscous (small couscous, not pearl), preferably a boxed roasted-garlic variety

¼ cup (65 g) sliced dried apricots and ¼ cup (73 g) dried raisins

1½ tablespoons Spice Mix #1 (page 38)

½ teaspoon salt

1 pouch pitted green olives, approximately 2½ ounces (70 g)

½–¾ cup (56–84 g) toasted chopped pecans or almonds

1 tablespoon (15 ml) oil

1 packet (1 g) True Lemon (crystallized lemon)

Tuna, salmon, or chicken from a pouch (optional)

MAKE IT

1. To make the mix, combine the couscous, the spice pack from the couscous box, dried fruit, spice mix, and salt in a sealable container.

2. To prepare, bring about 5 ounces (150 ml) of water to boil in a pot. Stir in the couscous mixture, remove from the heat, cover, and let stand for 5 minutes.

3. Stir in the olives, pecans, oil, and True Lemon (and a pouch of protein, if using). Serve!

DON'T FORGET SOME STURDY FRESH FRUITS AND VEGGIES

One of the things that can wear on you when you're on trail is the absence of really fresh-tasting foods, an unavoidable fact since you are carrying your food without refrigeration and with pack weight concerns. But unless you are an ultralight hiker who is managing your food weight to the milligram, you may decide you can make room and opportunity to pack a few fresh fruits and vegetables with you, if you choose wisely. Opt for fruits and vegetables that don't bruise or smash easily, are durable, and have minimal nonedible parts like peels or husks. Some good options are carrots, snap peas, cauliflower florets, apples, and clementines. Remember, you probably won't want to use your water to wash fruit or veggies on trail, so wash them at home before packing.

FALAFEL PATTY MIX

MAKES 5-6 SERVINGS

I remember when my family first discovered falafel. Being from Norway, falafel was *wayyyy* outside our traditional food rotation. But my mom found a packaged falafel mix in the grocery store and decided to give it a try. We were instantly hooked by the crispy patties, heady with earthy spices like cumin and coriander. When I started cooking for myself in college, I had falafel mix weekly. You can buy a prepackaged falafel mix, but it's not too hard to mix up your own batch, which also allows you to adjust the spice blend at will. The lightweight blend of chickpea flour and spices is easy to pack and full of protein. The only tricky bit is that patties of any sort don't love to stay in patty form while frying if you haven't refrigerated them, which simply isn't an option on trail. But I don't think any of us are that picky about the exact shape of our food at the end of a big day of being outside, now are we?

INGREDIENTS

FOR THE MIX

5 cups (460 g) chickpea flour

2 tablespoons (3 g) dried parsley

1 tablespoon (18 g) salt

1 tablespoon (7 g) ground cumin

1 tablespoon (6 g) ground coriander

1 tablespoon (9 g) garlic powder

½ tablespoon (3 g) ground
black pepper

½ teaspoon cayenne (optional)

2 teaspoons (2 g) dried dill
(or replace the dried parsley
and dill with 3 tablespoons
of Spice Mix #2 on page 39)

2 teaspoons (10 g) baking powder

FOR COOKING

True Lemon packets (1 for each 1-cup
serving you plan to prepare)

Cooking oil

Pita bread

Sun-dried tomatoes

Veggie chips

Mayonnaise packets

MAKE IT

1. Combine all the mix ingredients, whisking to combine well. Store in an airtight container.

2. To prepare 1 serving of falafel, add 1 cup of the mixture to a bowl and stir in 1 packet of True Lemon. Heat ½ cup water (120 ml) until hot but not boiling. Stir the water into the falafel mixture and allow to stand for about 15 minutes.

3. Heat a cooking pan over medium-high heat and add enough oil to coat the pan well. Use your hands or a spoon to scoop the falafel mixture into small patties (1 cup of the mixture should make about 5) and fry the patties in the oil until well browned (about 2 minutes) on the first side. Flip and cook on the other side. Because you won't be able to refrigerate the patties on trail before frying, they may have a tendency to fall apart. It's okay. Crispy falafel bits still taste good.

4. Serve with pita bread plus some lightweight veggies (like sun-dried tomatoes and veggie chips). To stand in for a tahini sauce, add a little pack of mayo as well, as though it were an aioli.

CHAPTER THREE

FLASK COCKTAILS

When you are out on trail, you're not likely to be in party mode. But, perhaps you still want to treat yourself to a sip of a celebratory cocktail after a successful (or just long) day on the trail. One of the tastiest and most expeditious ways of doing so is having a cocktail that you prepared at home and brought in a flask with you! Do the work at home and reap the rewards in camp.

PACKING A FLASK

The thing that is so nice about flask cocktails is that you can use multiple bottles and measuring utensils that you have at home, then funnel it into a flask to carry with you while leaving all those bottles and measuring utensils behind. By "flask," I mean any container made to carry liquid and seal well. You could use an actual flask, but if you prefer you could also use a water bottle, thermos, or a plastic reservoir used in hydration packs. Whatever you choose for transporting your cocktail of choice, here are a few flask-building principles to abide by.

1. **Use good-quality spirits.** Yes, you might be able to chill your flask cocktail in a cool lake or a snowbank depending on when and where you are camping, but you should be prepared to drink your cocktail at the ambient air temperature; at warmer temperatures any harshness or imbalance in the booze becomes more apparent.

2. **Opt for an aged spirit as your base spirit.** This is not a hard-and-fast rule. Some people may be totally happy to have a gin cocktail from a flask, but I find that aged spirits (a.k.a. brown spirits) are softer and rounder in flavor from the process of aging in oak, and this makes them more pleasant at room temperature.

3. **Choose a "stirred" cocktail recipe.** You want to choose a recipe with all booze-based ingredients. A syrup is okay, but I mainly opt for recipes that call for liqueurs instead of syrups. Avoid citrus, dairy, and egg. You want all of the ingredients in your cocktail to be super stable so that they don't degrade over the time spent together in the flask and at room temperature.

4. **Choose a recipe that is interesting but that you'll be happy sipping several nights in a row.** I say choose something interesting because you want your flask cocktails to be complex enough, even challenging enough, that they give you a full sensory experience with just a few sips. Why? Because you're out on the trail, working hard, making good decisions, and being safe, and this is not the time to go crazy, even once your tent is staked for the night. I always choose a cocktail that is on the bitter and moody side for that reason. That said, you don't want to fill a flask to last four nights only to find that after one night of enjoying your dram you're totally over it and wishing for something else.

5. **Do some math!** You can convert any recipe to fit any size carrying vessel with a little math. Get ready to become friends with ratios and percentages. The basic method is to add up all of the individual ingredient volumes to get the total volume of one serving. If you want to have your cocktail prediluted, which I recommend because it really helps with softening and opening up the flavors of the drink, calculate 20 to 25 percent of the cocktail volume. That's your water volume. Add this to the total volume. Then use this new total volume to figure out how many times you need to multiply your recipe to fit the size container you want to use.

Also, bitters don't always scale proportionally. The bigger the batch, the less predictable it is. When I multiply a recipe, I start by using only half the amount of bitters that I calculate and then add more to taste. Got that? Me either.

Let's practice some batching math. Start with a Manhattan. The recipe I like to use is 2½ ounces (75 ml) whiskey, 1 ounce (30 ml) sweet vermouth, and 2 dashes of bitters. Thus, 2½ + 1 = 3½ ounces (105 ml) total; the bitters don't count toward the volume because the amounts are too small. Next, 20 percent of 3½ ounces (105 ml) is 0.7 ounce (21 ml), which is an awkward amount, so we will up that slightly to 0.75 (or ¾) ounce (23 ml) of water. Add this in and your total volume of the finished cocktail is 4¼ ounces (128 ml). If you have an 8-ounce (240 ml) flask, you won't be able to quite fit two servings of cocktail. You can deal with this in two potential ways. The easiest thing to do is make a double batch (5 ounces [150 ml] whiskey, 2 ounces [60 ml] sweet vermouth, 4 dashes of bitters, and 1½ ounces [45 ml] water), funnel what fits into your flask, and then save or drink the small amount remaining. Or you could make a one and three-quarters batch, in which case you would multiply each of the ingredient amounts by 1.75 and deal with the awkward amounts. See, this is why I put that exclamation point after "do some math!" Phew. Don't worry. I'll also give you batch measurements in the recipes in this chapter.

FLASK OLD-FASHIONED

Year after year, season after season, the old-fashioned is the top seller at the bar at the distillery I own. The appeal of this cocktail is clearly undeniable. The old-fashioned really epitomizes what good cocktails are all about: good ingredients adding up to more than the sum of their parts. In this case, the simple combination of whiskey, sugar, and bitters is balanced, satisfying, and enduring.

INGREDIENTS

FOR 1 COCKTAIL

2 ounces (60 ml) whiskey

1 teaspoon simple syrup

3–4 dashes Angostura bitters

FOR AN 8-OUNCE (240 ML) FLASK

6 ounces (180 ml) whiskey

3 teaspoons simple syrup

12 dashes Angostura bitters

1¾ ounces (53 ml) water

FOR A 32-OUNCE (960 ML) WATER BOTTLE

3 cups (710 ml) whiskey

2 ounces (60 ml) simple syrup

About 5 teaspoons Angostura bitters

7 ounces (210 ml) water

MAKE IT

FOR 1 COCKTAIL

Combine all the ingredients in a stirring glass and add ice. Stir to chill, then strain into a lowball glass over an ice cube.

FOR AN 8-OUNCE (240 ML) FLASK

Stir all the ingredients together in a small pitcher or measuring cup. Funnel all that fits into a flask. You should have just a wee bit left over to sip as a treat for doing such a good job making a flask cocktail.

FOR A 32-OUNCE (960 ML) WATER BOTTLE

Stir all the ingredients together in a pitcher. Pour all, or all that fits, into the water bottle.

APPLE NEGRONI

The Negroni was the cocktail that first made me fall in love with craft cocktails. I've loved Campari since, well, since an earlier age than was appropriate for me to love Campari. And the combination of gin, Campari, and sweet vermouth is undeniably a classic. It's also undeniably not very good at room temperature. I keep trying flask Negronis, but they are always a disappointment. The interplay of gin and Campari is too harsh when it isn't perfectly chilled. So what's a Negroni-loving girl to do for her camping trips? The solution is simple: make one of the many Negroni variations that use an aged base spirit. This particular variation uses apple brandy as the base spirit, which makes for a lusciously soft cocktail without being overtly fruity.

INGREDIENTS

FOR 1 COCKTAIL

2 ounces (60 ml) Calvados or apple brandy

1 ounce (30 ml) Campari

1 ounce (30 ml) sweet vermouth

1 ounce (30 ml) water

FOR AN 8-OUNCE (240 ML) FLASK

3½ ounces (105 ml) Calvados or apple brandy

1¾ ounces (53 ml) Campari

1¾ ounces (53 ml) sweet vermouth

1¾ ounces (53 ml) water

FOR A 32-OUNCE (960 ML) WATER BOTTLE

12½ ounces (375 ml) Calvados or apple brandy

6¼ ounces (188 ml) Campari

6¼ ounces (188 ml) sweet vermouth

6¼ ounces (188 ml) water

MAKE IT

FOR 1 COCKTAIL

Combine all the ingredients in a stirring glass and add ice. Stir to chill, then strain into a lowball glass over an ice cube.

FOR AN 8-OUNCE (240 ML) FLASK

Stir all the ingredients together in a small pitcher or measuring cup. Funnel all that fits into a flask. You should have just a wee bit left over to sip as a treat for doing such a good job making a flask cocktail.

FOR A 32-OUNCE (960 ML) WATER BOTTLE

Stir all the ingredients together in a pitcher. Pour all, or all that fits, into the water bottle.

SHETLAND SWEATER

Scotland is renowned for its whiskey. It is also renowned for inclement weather. My friend Dave once told me a story of hiking in Scotland through pelting rain and biting wind. As he struggled up a steep cliff, soaked with sweat and rain, he came upon a man strolling along buck naked but for a woolen cap and a sturdy umbrella. As their paths crossed, they had a brief, surprisingly cheerful interchange. Dave couldn't help but remark on the man's extremely, one could say excessively, natural state of dress. The man replied in a sage brogue, "There's nae escapin' the rain. In weather such as this ye can be wet inside and oot . . . or just oot." And away he went. There is wisdom in his words, but still, let us hope that after he returned to shelter, he warmed himself up with both a fuzzy sweater and a smooth, hearty cocktail like this one.

INGREDIENTS

FOR 1 COCKTAIL

1 ounce (30 ml) blended Scotch

½ ounce (15 ml) apple brandy

½ ounce (15 ml) Amaro Averna

½ ounce (15 ml) Amaro Nonino

½ teaspoon maple syrup

1 dash orange bitters

A generous ½ ounce (15 ml) water

FOR AN 8-OUNCE (240 ML) FLASK

3 ounces (90 ml) blended Scotch

1½ ounces (45 ml) apple brandy

1½ ounces (45 ml) Amaro Averna

1½ ounces (45 ml) Amaro Nonino

1½ teaspoons (8 ml) maple syrup

2 dashes orange bitters

1½ ounces (45 ml) water

FOR A 32-OUNCE (960 ML) WATER BOTTLE

10½ ounces (315 ml) blended Scotch

5¼ ounces (158 ml) apple brandy

5¼ ounces (158 ml) Amaro Averna

5¼ ounces (158 ml) Amaro Nonino

¾ ounce (23 ml) maple syrup

6 dashes orange bitter

5¼ ounces (158 ml) water

MAKE IT

FOR 1 COCKTAIL

Combine all the ingredients in a stirring glass and add ice. Stir to chill, then strain into a lowball glass over an ice cube.

FOR AN 8-OUNCE (240 ML) FLASK

Stir all the ingredients together in a small pitcher or measuring cup. Funnel all that fits into a flask. You should have just a wee bit left over to sip as a treat for doing such a good job making a flask cocktail.

FOR A 32-OUNCE (960 ML) WATER BOTTLE

Stir all the ingredients together in a pitcher. Pour all, or all that fits, into the water bottle.

TIP

My go-to apple brandy for this cocktail is Laird's Straight Apple Brandy.

FLASK MANHATTAN

I have a deep affection for Manhattans, even the bad ones. It is my lazy evening cocktail, the only cocktail I make without measuring because I like the combination of whiskey and vermouth (plus a dash of bitters) in any proportion. It is a winning combo. The Manhattan debuted on the cocktail scene in the 1870s and has reigned, unquestioned and timeless, ever since. While I am an equal opportunity Manhattan drinker, some renditions are discernably better than others, and because you're going to the trouble of preparing a flask ahead of time, why not have the best?

INGREDIENTS

FOR 1 COCKTAIL

2½ ounces (75 ml) rye or bourbon whiskey

1 ounce (30 ml) sweet vermouth

2 dashes Angostura bitters

¾ ounce (23 ml) water

FOR AN 8-OUNCE (240 ML) FLASK

5 ounces (150 ml) whiskey

2 ounces (60 ml) sweet vermouth

4 dashes Angostura bitters

1½ ounces (45 ml) water

FOR A 32-OUNCE (960 ML) WATER BOTTLE

18¾ ounces (563 ml) whiskey

7½ ounces (225 ml) sweet vermouth

10 dashes Angostura bitters

5½ ounces (165 ml) water

MAKE IT

FOR 1 COCKTAIL

Combine all the ingredients in a stirring glass and add ice. Stir to chill, then strain into a lowball glass over an ice cube.

FOR AN 8-OUNCE (240 ML) FLASK

Stir all the ingredients together in a small pitcher or measuring cup. Funnel all that fits into a flask. You should have just a wee bit left over to sip as a treat for doing such a good job making a flask cocktail.

FOR A 32-OUNCE (960 ML) WATER BOTTLE

Stir all the ingredients together in a pitcher. Pour all, or all that fits, into the water bottle.

FLASK DUKE

Apple brandy, though relatively unused compared to many other spirits in cocktails, is one of my favorite spirits for outdoor tipples. It's rich and fruity but not sweet and gives a pleasant fall touch to any drink. In this cocktail we balance it out with cognac and give it a dark, moody, and aromatic twist with Amaro and Bénédictine, a honeyed herbal liqueur.

INGREDIENTS

FOR 1 COCKTAIL

1 ounce (30 ml) cognac

¾ ounce (23 ml) apple brandy

¼ ounce (8 ml) Amaro Montenegro

¼ ounce (8 ml) Bénédictine

2 dashes Angostura bitters

FOR AN 8-OUNCE (240 ML) FLASK

2½ ounces (75 ml) cognac

A scant 2 ounces (60 ml) apple brandy

½ ounce plus ¾ teaspoon (18 ml) Amaro Montenegro

½ ounce plus ¾ teaspoon (18 ml) Bénédictine

5 dashes Angostura bitters

1¾ ounces (53 ml) water

FOR A 32-OUNCE (960 ML) WATER BOTTLE

10 ounces (300 ml) cognac

7½ ounces (225 ml) apple brandy

2½ ounces (75 ml) Amaro Montenegro

2½ ounces (75 ml) Bénédictine

18 dashes Angostura bitters

5 ounces (150 ml) water

MAKE IT

FOR 1 COCKTAIL

Stir all the ingredients in a mixing glass with ice until chilled. Strain into a cocktail coupe.

FOR AN 8-OUNCE (240 ML) FLASK

Stir all the ingredients together in a measuring cup or small pitcher and funnel into a flask.

FOR A 32-OUNCE (960 ML) WATER BOTTLE

Stir all the ingredients together in a large measuring cup or pitcher and pour into a water bottle.

FLASK RED RUM

This is a spin-off of a cocktail called the Preakness, which is itself a spin-off of a Manhattan. Don't let the spinning make you dizzy; it's really a lovely balance of sweet and stiff between the spirits, vermouth, and liqueur. What makes it special is the rum and Tiki bitters, which give it a hint of the tropics. Just the smallest whiff of beachy escapism while you are on trail, you might say.

INGREDIENTS

FOR 1 COCKTAIL

1 ounce (30 ml) rye whiskey

1 ounce (30 ml) aged rum

¾ ounce (23 ml) sweet vermouth

¼ ounce (8 ml) Bénédictine

4 dashes Tiki bitters

FOR AN 8-OUNCE (240 ML) FLASK

2 ounces (60 ml) rye whiskey

2 ounces (60 ml) aged rum

1½ ounces (45 ml) sweet vermouth

½ ounce (15 ml) Bénédictine

8 dashes Tiki bitters

1 ounce (30 ml) water

FOR A 32-OUNCE (960 ML) WATER BOTTLE

8 ounces (240 ml) rye whiskey

8 ounces (240 ml) aged rum

6 ounces (180 ml) sweet vermouth

2 ounces (60 ml) Bénédictine

5 teaspoons Tiki bitters

4 ounces (120 ml) water

MAKE IT

FOR 1 COCKTAIL

Stir all the ingredients in a mixing glass with ice until chilled. Strain into a cocktail coupe. If desired, garnish with a lemon twist.

FOR AN 8-OUNCE (240 ML) FLASK

Stir all the ingredients together in a measuring cup or small pitcher and funnel into a flask.

FOR A 32-OUNCE (960 ML) WATER BOTTLE

Stir all the ingredients together in a large measuring cup or pitcher and pour into a water bottle.

ABOUT BÉNÉDICTINE

One of my favorite flask cocktail ingredients, Bénédictine is an herbal liqueur from France, originally created in the nineteenth century by a Benedictine monk. The exact recipe for Bénédictine is a closely guarded secret, but it has a richly complex flavor redolent with honey, citrus, herbs, and spices—all characteristics I really like in my campsite cocktails.

CHAPTER FOUR

EASY TO ASSEMBLE

Easy-to-assemble meals are precisely that: easy to throw together and perfect for when you don't want to stop for long, if at all. These recipes include wraps and sandwiches that are ideal for filling you up without slowing you down.

MATPAKKE

SERVES 1

Hold tight because I'm about to dump you into the middle of an ongoing marital dispute. By way of important context, my mom is from Norway, and I grew up spending all of my summers in Norway. In Norway, both breakfasts and lunches tend to be an open-faced sandwich, a simple slice of bread with butter and either cheese or meat (occasionally both), plus a couple of vegetable slices. If you will be having lunch on the go, you make a *matpakke*—literally a "food pack"—toward the end of eating breakfast. When you're Norwegian, there are strict rules about the "right" way to do things, and this goes for making a *matpakke* as much as for anything else. You make yourself two open-faced sandwiches, then you stack them—face-to-face—and wrap them in paper to transport them. My husband insists, repeatedly and volubly, that these stacked open-faced sandwiches are "just a sandwich" and that it is unreasonable to say otherwise. He is wrong. It is a *matpakke*. It is two open-faced sandwiches, and you must disassemble them before eating them!

INGREDIENTS

2 slices of good, crusty whole-grain bread

European butter

1–2 ounces (28–55 g) Jarlsberg cheese, thinly sliced

1–2 slices red bell pepper

About 4 thin slices of good salami

A few very thin slices of cucumber

MAKE IT

1. Butter each slice of bread well, then top 1 of them with Jarlsberg and red pepper and the other with salami and cucumber. Put the 2 pieces of bread together as if you were making it all into a sandwich, but be aware, this is not a sandwich. It is a *matpakke*.

2. Wrap up your not-a-sandwich in brown paper or in a sealed container to bring with you wherever the morning may take you. To serve, take the 2 halves apart again so you have 1 open-faced sandwich with cheese and pepper and 1 with salami and cucumber. This is important because there is a right way and a wrong way to do things, and Norwegians do it the right way!

SUMMER SAUSAGE SANDWICH

SERVES 1

Other than peanut butter and jelly, this is by far the sandwich that comes to mind when I think of camping. The first time my friends and I ever went camping in the Boundary Waters Canoe Area in Minnesota with no adults (!), we used a packing list given to us by one of the dads. We followed it to the letter, which meant the only lunch options we had for the week were PB&J tortillas and summer sausage and cheese sandwiches. We had a fantastic trip, and nobody can prove it wasn't because of all the summer sausage.

INGREDIENTS

2 slices of your favorite sturdy, packable bread

2–3 ounces (57–85 g) of a packable hard sliced cheese, like cheddar

2 ounces (55 g) sliced summer sausage

MAKE IT

Layer the cheese and sausage on 1 slice of bread and top with the other. If you've brought mayo and mustard packets, smear your bread with those as well. That's it! In the words of my friend Haakon: "When I'm at home, summer sausage never sounds that good. But when I'm camping, I just really want summer sausage."

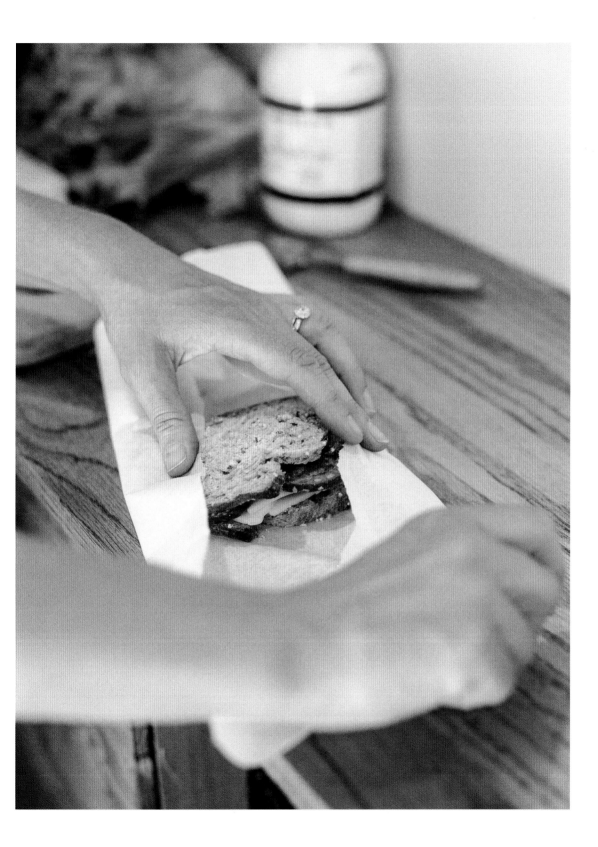

CURRIED TUNA WRAP

SERVES 1-2

I've always been a tuna salad person. It was my go-to order at Subway when I was a teenager, which is perhaps odd for a high schooler, but I could probably have been considered odd. Anyway, discovering curried tuna salad blew all past tunas out of the water. The idea comes from a sandwich at Flour Bakery in Boston, but I've lopped off all the frills to make it suitable for making in camp.

INGREDIENTS

1 pouch (2.6 ounces/74 g) of tuna

2 packets (22 g) of mayonnaise

1 teaspoon curry powder

1 tablespoon (10 g) raisins or golden raisins

1–2 flour tortillas

MAKE IT

1. Open the tuna pouch, add in the mayonnaise and curry powder, and mix it up with a camping fork or spork. Add in the raisins and mix a bit more.

2. Scoop the tuna mixture out onto the tortilla(s), roll up, and eat!

ALMOND BUTTER WRAP WITH DRIED FRUIT AND CINNAMON

SERVES 1

Maybe you noticed right away, maybe you didn't, but I'll go ahead and fess up anyway: This is just a glorified peanut butter and jelly wrap. It takes the most stalwart of all trail lunches and gives it a wee twist, swapping peanut butter for almond butter and messy jelly for tidily packaged dried fruit. Then it makes it all fragrant and fancy with a pinch of cinnamon.

INGREDIENTS

1 flour tortilla

1–2 tablespoons (16–32 g) salted almond butter (if you have unsalted almond butter, sprinkle a nice pinch of salt over yours after spreading)

1–2 tablespoons (15–30 g) of your choice of dried fruit (I recommend Craisins or chopped dried figs)

A pinch of cinnamon

MAKE IT

Spread the almond butter on the tortilla, and sprinkle over dried fruit and a pinch of cinnamon. Roll up and enjoy.

TIP

This will work with any nut butter, or even with tahini (adding a pinch or two of salt is a must!) or sunflower seed butter.

BAGEL WITH APPLE AND PEANUT BUTTER AND RAISINS

SERVES 1-2

This quick lunch idea takes everyone's favorite afternoon snack (apple slices with peanut butter and raisins) and piles it on top of a bagel for extra energy. Easy peasy packable silicone tube of peanut butter squeezy!

INGREDIENTS

1 plain bagel

1–2 tablespoons (16–32 g) peanut butter

1 tablespoon (10 g) raisins

¼ of an apple, thinly sliced

MAKE IT

Split the bagel in half and spread each half with peanut butter. Sprinkle raisins on each half and top with apple slices. Enjoy open-faced.

A CARBY DISCUSSION

Bringing good sources of carbohydrates is important for keeping your muscles fueled for active days on the trail. And different packable carbs have different packing perks. When it comes to easy-to-prepare, sandwich-like meals, you can choose from bread, tortillas, bagels, and crackers, to name a few.

- Crackers are tricky because they break easily. Make sure to pack them in a hard-sided container if you are bringing them so you don't find yourself sadly staring at a pile of crumbs a couple days in.

- Bagels give you the highest density of food, the most carb bang for your buck, if you will, and they are hard to destroy. But some people don't love untoasted bagels, so I'll leave it as your personal decision whether or not to bring them.

- Tortillas are great because they don't take up much space, and you literally can't squash them because they are already flat.

- You truly can't beat bread for a sandwich. But a bread loaf is bulky and a little easier to squish than bagels and tortillas, so pack with care.

Don't Forget Protein

While carbs will keep you going, some solid sources of protein are also important to include in your day. Protein will keep you feeling full, help muscles recover, and bolster your immune system, among other things. Some of the best lightweight and packable proteins include:

- Nuts and nut butters, which are a good source of protein along with healthy fats

- Beans in various forms

- Chicken, tuna, or salmon in pouches

- Jerky or other dehydrated meats

- Traditional cured meats like salami or summer sausage

- Hard cheeses or dehydrated cheese powders

FRIED WRAP À LA NORWEGIANS

SERVES 1

In Norwegian there's a well-known adage, *"Ut på tur, aldri sur."* This translates essentially to "It's impossible to be grumpy when you're out on the trail." But in Norwegian it rhymes. Norwegians are an outdoorsy bunch! And they are great at trail food. My personal favorite is the little grills and sausages that you bring on a long cross-country ski trip, but another fun Norwegian camp food specialty is souped-up versions of quesadillas or fried tortilla packets. Some of these wraps include sauces that I absolutely don't think belong, but this pesto and chicken variation is excellent.

INGREDIENTS

1 flour tortilla

1 tablespoon (15 g) basil pesto (you can buy prepared pesto and transfer it to a small container to pack; you may want to pack enough to use on some pasta as well!)

1 packet (2.6 ounces/74 g) of cooked chicken (such as a StarKist pouch)

2–3 tablespoons (10–15 g) grated hard cheese (like Parmesan or cheddar)

Butter or oil for frying

MAKE IT

1. Spread the pesto on the tortilla. Pile the chicken and cheese in the middle of the tortilla in a square shape. Fold the top and the bottom of the tortilla over to meet in the middle. Then fold the sides in over the top and bottom, a bit like making a flatter burrito.

2. Heat a cooking pan over medium-low heat, and add butter (or oil) and melt. Carefully add the wrap, folded side down. Cook until that side is golden brown and the cheese is sort of starting to melt. (Hard cheese doesn't love melting. But it also doesn't need refrigeration. So, trade-offs, I guess!) Flip and cook the other side until golden brown and the wrap is warmed through the middle. The cook time is going to depend a lot on your camp stove, but it should be a couple minutes per side. Eat warm.

CHAPTER FIVE

JUST ADD ____

Some things are staples for a reason, but that doesn't mean you can't get jazzy with them. These simple recipes take some of the classic prepared camping foods and zhoosh them up with a little something-something to make them feel like brand-new. They don't reinvent the wheel, but they do add some really cool lights and streamers to the spokes.

(POWDERED) EGG SCRAMBLE

SERVES 2

I like to start my day savory. On any given day you are far more likely to find me eating fish, eggs, or an avocado for breakfast than a smoothie or cereal. This remains true when I'm camping. When I have my druthers, a rib-sticking, salty, punchy breakfast is the name of the game. And nothing fits the bill better than an egg scramble. If I'm honest, dehydrated egg powder is kind of weird, but if you add some cheese and veggies and wrap it in a tortilla, it becomes entirely respectable.

INGREDIENTS

¾ cup (84 g) dehydrated egg powder

1 tablespoon (16 g) heavy cream powder

½ cup (10 g) dehydrated spinach

½ teaspoon salt

¼ teaspoon Spice Mix #3 (page 39), optional

1 tablespoon (15 ml) olive oil or butter

2 tablespoons (10 g) grated Parmesan

2 flour or corn tortillas

MAKE IT

1. Combine the egg powder, heavy cream powder, spinach, salt, and spice mix (if using) with 1⅓ cups (316 ml) water and whisk well until there are no lumps. Allow to stand for about 3 minutes.

2. Add the oil or butter to a small pan or pot over medium heat. Add the egg mixture and cook, stirring constantly, until it is cooked through and gently set. Remove from the heat and stir in the Parmesan.

3. Divide the egg scramble between the 2 tortillas and serve.

TIP

Better-quality powdered eggs have come out in recent years than were traditionally available. OvaEasy Egg Crystals are one of the best.

COCONUT OATMEAL BOWL

SERVES 1

If you like to start your day with something warm that requires very minimal time and effort, instant oatmeal is the breakfast for you. It will stick to your ribs, and it works as a blank canvas for any topping you can imagine, sweet or savory. This variation is a tropical medley in a bowl with sweet dried tropical fruit and aromatic coconut.

INGREDIENTS

1 packet (1.8 ounces/50 g) plain instant oatmeal

1 tablespoon (5 g) dried coconut milk

1 tablespoon (6 g) toasted shredded coconut

2 tablespoons (30 g) chopped dried tropical fruit such as pineapple, mango, kiwi, or guava (or a mix)

MAKE IT

1. Combine the instant oatmeal and dried coconut milk in a bowl. Pour about ½ cup (120 ml) boiling water over, stir, and allow to sit for 1 minute.

2. Top with shredded coconut and dried fruit, and enjoy.

TIP

As I mentioned, oatmeal can be topped with virtually anything you are in the mood for that you've packed with you. Try other combinations like banana chips and a spoonful of peanut butter, dried blueberries and chopped almonds or pecans, or dried strawberries and freeze-dried yogurt drops as just a few options.

TUNA CASSEROLE

SERVES 2

I'd be lying if I tried to pretend that we didn't mostly just eat mac 'n' cheese when we are camping. It's easy and delicious and omnipresent at our mealtimes. But one thing we do is mix in different things. Dumping in tuna and pretending it is a tuna casserole has been my favorite. Maybe it's just the hunger from being on the go and outside, but I swear it really does taste similar to a classic tuna noodle casserole, and it is certainly warm and comforting.

INGREDIENTS

1 6–7 ounce box (170–200 g) of macaroni and cheese

¼ cup (12 g) dried peas

1–2 tablespoons (5–10 g) dried milk powder

2 tablespoons (28 g) butter

1 packet (2.6 ounces/74 g) of tuna

MAKE IT

1. Bring a pot of water to a boil. Stir in the noodles and dried peas. Cook for the amount of time called for on the macaroni and cheese package.

2. Strain the noodles partway, leaving about ¼ cup of the pasta water in the pot with the pasta and peas. Then add in the cheese packet that came with the noodles, plus the milk powder and butter. Stir until creamy and well combined.

3. Add the tuna from the pouch. Use a fork to break it apart and gently fold it into the prepared noodles. Enjoy!

TIP

This is also tasty if you replace the tuna with slices of a preserved smoked sausage like summer sausage, conjuring the childhood staple of mac 'n' cheese with hot dogs.

CACIO E PEPE

SERVES 2

If I ever find myself with a culinary quandary (usually "What should I cook?" or "How many pasta meals is too many pasta meals?"), my go-to way to solve it is to ask myself, *What would an Italian eat?* It never steers me wrong. Cacio e pepe is a classic and minimal pasta dish from the region around Rome. Its pared-down ingredients—pasta, butter, lots of cheese and pepper—make it as speedy as it is delicious. One stumbling block, however, is the traditional process of vigorously stirring cheese and pasta water together a wee bit at a time to ensure a creamy noodle-coating sauce. Save that for your home kitchen. While camping we are going to circumvent this step by using packaged fettuccine Alfredo. (Yes, this bastardizes the dish. We can deal. Plus packaged fettuccine Alfredo is one of my secret pleasures even when I'm not on trail.)

INGREDIENTS

About 10 ounces (280 g) packaged dried fettuccine Alfredo

¾ cup (75 g) shaved or grated Parmesan

1 teaspoon coarsely ground black pepper

MAKE IT

1. Prepare the fettuccine Alfredo according to the package directions.

2. Stir in the Parmesan and black pepper until fully combined. Serve!

RICE NOODLES WITH PEANUT SAUCE

SERVES 2

Rice noodles are another quick cooking all-star, needing just a speedy bath in boiling water to be ready to eat. They are also a blank canvas to soak up any sauce you want to throw at them. But a sweet-savory spork-licking-good peanut sauce is one of the most satisfying options around.

INGREDIENTS

¼ cup (65 g) creamy peanut butter

1 tablespoon (15 ml) soy sauce (from 2 packets)

1 tablespoon (15 ml) rice wine vinegar

1 tablespoon (13–15 g) granulated sugar or brown sugar

½ teaspoon garlic powder

3 tablespoons (15 g) dried carrots and peas

6 ounces (180 g) vermicelli rice noodles

MAKE IT

1. Whisk the peanut butter, soy sauce, vinegar, sugar, and garlic powder together. Stir in water a spoonful at a time to reach a sauce consistency.

2. Bring a pot of water to a boil with the dried veggies in it, add the rice noodles, and remove from the heat. Allow to sit for about 3 minutes, until softened; then drain. Toss the noodle mixture with the sauce mixture.

TIP

For added flavor, you can stir in a packet of True Lime crystallized lime juice (or squeeze in a lime wedge if you've packed some fresh citrus). You can also drizzle with sriracha or chili garlic sauce from a packet to add spice.

HERBED BEANS WITH SALAMI

SERVES 1-2

If we are abiding by the "What would an Italian eat?" rule of thumb (see the Cacio e Pepe recipe on page 90 if you're like, "What is she talking about?"), we will not go for austerity when it comes to beans. We will add fatty, salty pieces of meat and fragrant garlic and herbs. Perfectly rustic, hearty, and comforting.

INGREDIENTS

⅓ cup dehydrated white beans (not uncooked white beans, but camper's beans that have been cooked and then dehydrated)

¼ cup (49 g) instant rice

2 teaspoons Spice Mix #2 (page 39)

1 packet (0.64 ounce/20 g) chicken broth powder

¼ teaspoon salt, plus more to taste

1–2 ounces (28–55 g) hard salami, chopped into small bits

1 tablespoon (15 ml) olive oil

MAKE IT

Combine the beans, rice, spice mix, chicken broth powder, and salt in a pot. Add 1 cup (235 ml) of water and bring to a boil, stirring to dissolve the broth powder. Once the pot comes to a boil, remove from the heat. Let it sit until the beans and rice have softened, about 5 minutes. Stir in the salami bits and olive oil. Add more salt, if desired. Feel free to also add some Parmesan if you have it packed.

TIP

You can use other types of hard-cured sausage, like chorizo or pepperoni, to bring in different flavor and a bit of spice.

LENTIL "SHEPHERD'S PIE"

SERVES 1-2

Dehydrated soups are wonderfully convenient, but they often leave us feeling still kind of hungry unless we bulk them out. This preparation draws on the idea of shepherd's pie, which is a hearty stew topped with mashed potatoes. You could use a dehydrated beef stew as the stew portion, but using a lentil soup is a nice vegetarian option!

INGREDIENTS

½ cup (29 g) butter-flavored instant mashed potatoes

1 teaspoon Spice Mix #2 (page 39)

1 package (4 ounces/115 g) dehydrated lentil soup

Salt to taste

MAKE IT

1. Place the instant mashed potatoes and spice mix in a container. Bring 1 cup (235 ml) of water to a boil and pour it over the potato mix. Stir and set aside.

2. Prepare the lentil soup according to the package directions but with only three-fourths the amount of water so it is a little more stewy.

3. Add more salt to the potatoes, if necessary. Then top the lentils with the mashed potatoes and serve as a shepherd's pie.

TIP

Instant mashed potatoes make a nicely filling side for all sorts of bean dishes. Or make a quick chicken version of shepherd's pie by sautéing a packet of chicken with rehydrated vegetables in oil or butter and topping with instant mashed potatoes.

SALMON (PACKET) PATTIES

SERVES 1-2

Salmon cakes are a staple of our diet at home. And because you can conveniently get pouches of cooked flaked salmon, they can also be a simple, healthy, and satisfying meal on the trail. I have always used potato flakes as the binder in my salmon cakes. I think they taste better and have better texture than bread crumbs—and it makes them gluten-free if that is a need you have! But if you prefer bread or cracker crumbs, go ahead and use those instead of potato flakes.

INGREDIENTS

About 5 ounces (140 g) salmon from pouches (usually this is 2 pouches)

3 tablespoons (42 g) mayonnaise (4 little packets)

1 teaspoon Spice Mix #2 (page 39)

¼ teaspoon salt

¼ cup (14 g) dried potato flakes

Butter or oil for frying

MAKE IT

1. Remove the salmon from the pouches and put into a bowl. Add the mayonnaise, spice mix, salt, and potato flakes, and stir well with a fork to blend.

2. Allow the mixture to sit for about 5 minutes. Then form into 4 small patties.

3. Heat a frying pan over medium heat and add enough butter or oil to coat your pan well (about 1 tablespoon). Add the patties and fry until they are golden brown on the first side, about 4 minutes. Flip and fry until the other sides are browned. Transfer to plates and enjoy. You can make these into sandwiches or wraps by serving them on bread or tortilla, spread with a bit more mayo. If you pack sriracha packets to stir into the mayo, this is extra tasty for topping!

ON THE TRAIL ARSENAL—PACKING SAUCES AND CONDIMENTS

When you're out there on the trail, a little burst of flavor can make all the difference. So pack smart, pack flavorful, and let your culinary spirit soar, even in the great outdoors. Oils, condiments, and nut butters are all liquid-y and potentially messy ingredients, but in my opinion they are an absolute must to keep trail food edible. Luckily there are some easy packing tips that will help you haul everything from mayo to your favorite hot sauce, because we all know a powdered egg scramble is infinitely better with a drizzle of hot sauce.

For packing things like oils and condiments that are temperature stable (such as mustard, peanut butter, and so on), tiny, leak-proof containers are your best friend. Think about acquiring little travel-size bottles (for example, Nalgene makes some small, sturdy bottles)—they're a game changer. Fill them with your favorite ingredients, from olive oil to vinegar to soy sauce. Just ensure they're tight-sealed and won't explode in your bag. Nobody wants a surprise sriracha shower in the wilderness.

Another good bet is small silicone containers. Especially for the squishable stuff like ketchup or nut butters. They're flexible, lightweight, and virtually indestructible. Plus, they're a cinch to clean. Some even come in fun colors.

Last but not least, consider snagging single-serving packets to use when backpacking. Not only are they premeasured, but they're also mess-free. Just tear and squeeze! I especially recommend restaurant-style packets for mayo because these are shelf stable. And packets are also a highly convenient way of carrying nut butters and sauces like soy sauce and sriracha. (I'm not saying you should ask for extra packets when you get takeout so you can hoard them for camping, but I'm also not *not* saying that.)

CHAPTER SIX

FOR YOUR SWEET TOOTH

I don't think an excuse is ever needed to have a little dessert, but if you were looking for one, being on the trail and burning all those extra calories sure is a good excuse to treat yourself.

SAUTÉED APPLES

SERVES 1-2

I love sizzling fruit in a skillet to make a speedy dessert. Almost any fruit works well, but apples are the only ones you're likely to pack in a backpack, and they are my favorite to sauté because they quickly sweeten and concentrate into an apple-pie-like treat.

INGREDIENTS

1 tablespoon (14 g) butter

1 large apple, cut into thin slices

1 teaspoon granulated sugar or brown sugar, if desired

MAKE IT

Heat the butter in a pan over medium-high heat. Add the apples and sugar, if using, and sauté, stirring frequently until they have started to soften and brown. Remove from the heat and eat warm.

TIP

If you brought with you a bit of ground cinnamon because you like it in your oatmeal, sprinkle the apple with a pinch to make this speedy dessert taste even more like pie.

CHOCOLATE-COVERED ALMONDS AND DRIED PEARS

SERVES 1

This isn't even really a recipe; it's just a great combination! There is no dried fruit that tastes more like candy than dried pears. Pair them (or should I say pear them?) with chocolate-covered almonds for a simple and portable treat inspired by the French dessert Poire Belle Hélène.

INGREDIENTS

2 slices of dried pear

A handful of chocolate-covered almonds

MAKE IT

Alternate bites!

TIP

Here are some other great combinations to eat by the handful:

- Dried figs and dark chocolate

- Toasted hazelnuts and milk chocolate

- Dried apricots, dark chocolate, and pistachios

- Trail mix that has chocolate in it!

INSTANT TIRAMISU

SERVES 4

Real tiramisu is an *undertaking* to say the least. I've only made it twice, and it was worth it, but zero things about it say "I would make a good camping dessert." However, the flavors and the general idea of the ingredients actually can be mimicked in the woods! All you need to be an on-trail pastry chef is a bit of imagination and some instant pudding and instant coffee to pour on top of chocolate crackers.

INGREDIENTS

1 5-ounce box (144 g) instant vanilla pudding

1 cup (125 g) whole milk powder

1 teaspoon instant ground coffee

1 teaspoon cocoa powder

Chocolate graham crackers to taste (about 2 dozen)

MAKE IT

1. At home, combine the instant vanilla pudding, milk powder, and instant coffee. Divide into 4 equal servings and place in sealable bags to pack.

2. To prepare, add 3 ounces (90 ml) of water per serving. Stir vigorously with a fork or shake in a sealed bottle for about 2 minutes. Then set aside to thicken (the pudding won't thicken as much as if you were setting it in a refrigerator, but putting the water bottle in a nearby cold-water source like a creek or lake will help the pudding thicken).

3. Sprinkle with cocoa powder and serve over pieces of chocolate graham crackers.

TRAIL-READY PAIN AU CHOCOLAT

SERVES 1

You're unlikely to bring a freshly baked *pain au chocolat* with you backpacking. (Although, maybe for the first day? That sounds kind of awesome, actually.) But the absence of *pain au chocolat* does not necessitate the absence of bread and chocolate. And bread and chocolate, it turns out, is an absolutely delicious treat unto itself. This simple dessert works like making a grilled cheese or quesadilla; you just replace the cheese with chocolate—*et voilà!*

INGREDIENTS

1 flour tortilla or 1 slice of bread, cut in half

About 3 tablespoons (35 g) chocolate chips or dark chocolate in small pieces

Butter or oil for cooking

Salt (optional)

MAKE IT

1. Lay out the tortilla or one of the half slices of bread and sprinkle the chocolate on it. Fold the tortilla in half, or top the bread with the other half slice.

2. Heat a pan over medium-low heat and add a splash of oil or a pat of butter. Place the tortilla or the chocolate sandwich in the pan. Cook until the underside is golden and crispy, then flip and cook on the other side. Hopefully the chocolate will be melted by then! If not, keep cooking, flipping frequently until the chocolate gets melty. If desired, sprinkle with a pinch of salt before eating.

WILD BERRY CRUMBLE

SERVES 1-2

You can't take me anywhere during berry season. Try as I might to be a serious hiker, if there are berries along the trail, I will be in the berry patch stuffing my face instead of making forward progress. The very best use of fresh wild berries is, in fact, stuffing your face in the moment. But if you have some modicum of self-control, you can also collect a small container's worth and make yourself this tasty and easy dessert once you've set up camp.

INGREDIENTS

1 cup (145 g) wild berries (blueberries, raspberries, blackberries, thimbleberries, whatever is growing where you are)

1–2 teaspoons (4–10 g) sugar of any sort (you can sweeten to taste)

¼ cup (110 g) granola

MAKE IT

1. In a small pot or pan over low heat, stir together the berries and sugar and gently cook until the berries are warm but haven't started to break down, just a couple of minutes.

2. Remove from the heat, top with granola, and enjoy.

TIP

If there are no wild berries where you are planning to be camping, or you're concerned about your identification skills and don't want to forage, you can make this dessert with freeze-dried berries. Replace the fresh berries with about 1½ ounces (42 g) of freeze-dried berries (blueberries or strawberries work especially well) and 6 to 8 ounces (175 to 240 ml) of water. Cook the berries until they have absorbed the water.

CHAPTER SEVEN

BACKPACKER'S BEVVIES

Make sure you're staying hydrated on trail! But once you hit your campsite and it's time to rest and stretch your legs, you may find you want to enjoy a little happy hour or nightcap moment. These wildly simple cocktail ideas are here to help.

TRUE LIME GIMLET

SERVES 1

The gimlet finds its origins in naval history. The British Royal Navy required their sailors to take a ration of lime juice to prevent scurvy. To make the lime juice more palatable, the seafarers added gin and sugar. Given that the sailors were almost certainly enjoying this concoction sans ice, I think that you too can enjoy an air-temperature gimlet while you are on trail. And be scurvy-free!

INGREDIENTS

2 ounces (60 ml) gin

3 packets (3 g) True Lime

1½ tablespoons (20 g) granulated sugar

2½ ounces (42 ml) water

MAKE IT

Shake all the ingredients together in a water bottle to combine and froth. Pour into a camp cup for sipping, or sip from the water bottle.

POWDERED TEA ARNIE PALMER

SERVES 1

What's tastier than iced tea and more refreshing than lemonade? An Arnold Palmer! Legend has it that the golfing legend Arnold Palmer invented the drink himself while on the course. When you find yourself secretly wishing you could hitch a ride on a golf cart for part of your hike, maybe it's a sign it's time to stop and revive yourself with an Arnie Palmer. This is a wonderful drink unspiked, but if you really need a pick-me-up, you can add a nip of a spirit like vodka, gin, or bourbon.

INGREDIENTS

2 teaspoons (8–10 g) powdered iced tea

2 teaspoons (8–10 g) lemonade powder

1½ ounces (42 ml) vodka, gin, or bourbon (optional)

8 ounces (240 ml) water

MAKE IT

Stir all the ingredients together in a cup until the powder dissolves. Enjoy!

ON THE TRAIL ARSENAL— INSTANT DRINKS

The most important drink you can have while on trail is water! Make sure you're aware of what your water sources will be and bring a reliable water purification so you can always stay hydrated. Once you know your water sources are secured, you can also bring a variety of lightweight instant drinks to keep things varied and to provide extra calories and electrolytes.

You may want to bring instant coffee, tea bags, powdered tea, lemonade, or fruit-flavored electrolyte drinks. Another of my favorite things to have are True Lemon and True Lime packets. These are crystallized versions of the citrus juices that make great replacements for the real things for both drinks and cooking. Of course, if you are able to carry a bit of extra weight, real citrus is extremely tidy and sturdy to pack, so you could bring actual lemons and limes instead.

With an arsenal of beverages, you also have the option of bringing a wee flask of your favorite spirit if you want to treat yourself to the occasional little cocktail while you are jetboiling water for dinner or stretching your legs before bedtime. Just because you are on trail doesn't mean you have to be Spartan! Plus, as my friend Jake, who owns an outdoor guiding company, says, "When we pack for trips, we try to bring things that have at least two uses. And alcohol is also a disinfectant!"

SPIKED LEMONADE

SERVES 1

One of the watershed moments in cocktail-making history is when people started adding citrus to their mixtures of spirits and sugar. Call them daisies, call them sours, call them punch, they all branch from the same brilliant idea. You can celebrate the centuries of tradition while you're camping by shaking up a simple blend of citrus, sugar, water, and your preferred spirit. The adaptable nature of lemon makes it taste good with anything!

INGREDIENTS

3 packets (3 g) True Lemon or 1½ tablespoons (22 ml) lemon juice

1½ tablespoons (20 g) granulated sugar

2 ounces (60 ml) of your preferred spirit (gin, vodka, whiskey, rum— almost anything, really)

4–5 ounces (120–150 ml) water

MAKE IT

Shake everything together in a water bottle, or stir vigorously in a cup, and enjoy!

TIP

This is basically the same as mixing up some powdered lemonade and adding spirits. So, if you have brought lemonade powder, go ahead and use that instead of sugar and True Lemon.

INSTANT IRISH COFFEE

SERVES 1

While the true glory of a traditional Irish coffee is in the layer where cold whipped cream meets hot coffee, this is something we have to forgo when we are on trail because whipped cream is out of the picture. Lucky for us, the combination of strong coffee, bracing whiskey, and the sweetness of sugar is still a delight on its own.

INGREDIENTS

5 ounces (150 ml) strong hot coffee or 1 packet (28 g) of instant coffee mixed with 5 ounces (150 ml) hot water

1 tablespoon (15 g) brown sugar

1 ounce (30 ml) whiskey (Irish whiskey, of course, makes it most like an Irish coffee, but you can also use bourbon or a Highland— that is, not peaty—Scotch)

MAKE IT

Combine all the ingredients in a cup, stir well, and enjoy.

SPIKED HOT CHOCOLATE

SERVES 1

You'll never be without dessert on trail if you have hot cocoa with you. (I mean, as long as you have fuel for your camp stove. But that's a separate question of preparedness.) Even tastier if you gently spike it! Like a sweet symphony, cocoa harmonizes with lush oaked spirits or complexly bittersweet Amaro, making for an absolute treat.

INGREDIENTS

1 packet (39 g) hot cocoa mix

8 ounces (240 ml) hot water

1 ounce (30 ml) bourbon, brandy, aged rum, or minty Amaro like Nardini or Montenegro

MAKE IT

Combine all the ingredients in a cup, stir well, and enjoy.

SPIKED TEA

SERVES 1

A hot cuppa can be a soothing respite after a day of trekking, and most teas make a nice base for variations on the toddy. This one uses mint tea, which is wonderfully fragrant. And, when you combine it with sweetener and a bit of spirits, you will find yourself with something akin to a cozy warm version of a julep.

INGREDIENTS

1 tea bag (2 g) of mint tea

1 tablespoon (15 g) brown sugar or honey

1 ounce (30 ml) aged rum or bourbon

Pinch of cinnamon

MAKE IT

Steep the tea in 7 ounces (196 ml) of hot water for about 5 minutes. Remove the tea bag and stir in the brown sugar or honey, spirit, and pinch of cinnamon. If you would like, you can add a bit of True Lemon, or a squeeze of lemon juice, to taste.

TIP

Prefer a different type of tea or spirit? Try one of these other combinations: black tea and bourbon; chamomile tea and Highland Scotch; chai tea and rum. With any of these combinations I would definitely recommend adding True Lemon or lemon juice.

TODDLE OFF TODDY

SERVES 1

As with many traditional spirits and cocktails, the hot toddy was originally used as medicine. In the eighteenth century, it was common for physicians to prescribe a hot alcoholic beverage as a remedy for various ailments, particularly those associated with the cold and damp weather. So, if you're feeling a chill creeping into the air as you set up your tent for the night, you might want to concoct yourself a simple little toddy to properly warm you from the inside and relax you before you climb into your sleeping bag.

INGREDIENTS

2 packets (2 g) of True Lemon or 1½ tablespoons (22 ml) lemon juice

1–2 tablespoons (13–26 g) granulated sugar (to taste)

2 ounces (60 ml) whiskey of choice (I recommend bourbon)

4–5 ounces (112–140 ml) hot water (steaming, but not boiling)

MAKE IT

Combine the True Lemon and sugar in a camp cup and stir in the whiskey. Top with hot water and enjoy.

CHAPTER EIGHT

DEHYDRATOR TIDBITS

Water? Who needs it?! Just kidding—sort of. I mean, I did just spend no small amount of breath on the importance of hydration in the last section. But what you don't want is for water to be weighing down the ingredients in your food pack. Dehydrated food is super lightweight as well as quick cooking, making it one of the essential food groups of camping. You can purchase dehydrated ingredients, but it can also be fun—and surprisingly easy—to make your own.

DEHYDRATING OVERVIEW

Having a dehydrator is like having a magic trick for all things trail food related. Yes, it's just drying stuff. But drying stuff also makes it light! And shelf stable! And very packable. All things you want when you are out hiking. Dehydrated meals and ingredients are also very quick to prepare as you can usually just add some boiling water and allow them to sit. This saves time and cooking fuel.

Dehydrating is generally a very simple process. But there are a few basic rules that are important to apply:

1. Pick your produce. Choose good-quality fruits or veggies. If you are dehydrating a cooked meal or a jerky, make sure it's something that tastes great because the flavor will get locked in while drying.

2. Think thin and well prepared. Slice your fruits and veggies thinly. Blanch your veggies. Make sure your beans are fully cooked. Keep things thin, which will allow for faster drying times. Plus thin slices of dried fruits and veggies look like confetti, which is fun. Also, keep in mind that foods that are high in fat (avocado, nut butters, fatty sauces) do not dehydrate well.

3. Place things in the dehydrator with space to allow for good airflow. Different types of foods have different recommended dehydrating temperatures for food safety, so it's generally best to dehydrate ingredients in groups of similar things. The temperature recommendations are:

95°F (35°C)	Herbs
125°F (52°C)	Vegetables
125°F (52°C)	Beans and Lentils
135°F (57°C)	Fruit
145°F (63°C)	Grains
145°F (63°C)	Precooked Meats
160°F (71°C)	Meat, Seafood
165°F (74°C)	Poultry

Don't turn up the temperature to speed up drying times because too high of a temperature can cause the outside of a food to harden before all the moisture actually evaporates, so the ingredients can't fully dry.

4. If you are using a dehydrator with stacked trays, make sure to switch the order of the trays every so often to allow for even drying. Make sure you allow your food to dry fully. Cut or break pieces in half to check and make sure the middle is dried through. With veggies this means crispy; with fruits this usually means leathery (but, like, in a nice way).

DIY BEEF JERKY

SERVES 12

Dried meat is one of those things that you really shouldn't think too hard about. Once you start overthinking it, it seems like such a bad idea. But in fact, and on the contrary, drying meat is one of the oldest ways of preserving it and has given rise to exemplary charcuterie treats the likes of prosciutto and bresaola. Jerky is more utilitarian but no less iconic. And, while store-bought jerky is perfectly fine and I would not discourage you from stocking up, homemade jerky is actually much more cost-effective and not wildly difficult. The things to remember are: thin slices and excellent marinade. Here is a version with a fairly traditional and very flavorful marinade.

INGREDIENTS

3-pound (1.4 kg) eye of round roast

1 cup (240 g) packed dark brown sugar

1 cup (236 ml) soy sauce

3 tablespoons (45 ml) Worcestershire sauce

1 teaspoon smoked paprika

1 teaspoon unseasoned meat tenderizer (I use McCormick, which is easy to find in a regular grocery store in the spice section)

1 teaspoon freshly ground black pepper

½ teaspoon red pepper flakes

1 teaspoon onion powder

½ teaspoon garlic powder

SPECIAL EQUIPMENT

Food dehydrator

MAKE IT

1. Remove all the visible fat from the outside of the round roast, particularly any fat cap or silver skin. Then cut it very thinly (⅛ to ¼ inch [3 to 6 mm] thick) against the grain. You can ask your butcher to slice it for you if you are buying for one. Otherwise, to make cutting easier, freeze your hunk o' meat for an hour to make it cold and firm and easier to handle before thinly slicing.

2. In a large baking pan, whisk together the sugar, soy sauce, Worcestershire sauce, paprika, meat tenderizer, pepper, pepper flakes, and onion and garlic powders. Add the meat strips and toss them well to fully coat them with the marinade. Spread out into as close to a single layer as possible in the baking dish. Cover the dish tightly and place in the fridge. Allow to marinate for at least 12 hours.

3. Remove the meat strips from the marinade and shake off excess liquid. Then spread the meat in single layers on your dehydrator trays. Dry at 160˚F (74˚C) until dried, about 4 to 6 hours. (Jerky can also be spread onto work racks and dried in the oven. Use a 175˚F [80˚C] oven and dry for about 3 to 4 hours.) Occasionally blot off any fat that beads to the surface of the meat as it dries. To test a piece for dryness, remove it from the dehydrator and allow it to cool to room temperature. Then bend it to see if it cracks but does not break. Done jerky should feel dry and leathery but still tender enough to chew.

4. Allow all of your finished jerky to cool, then store in an airtight container in a dark, cool place until ready to use or pack.

DEHYDRATED STRAWBERRIES AND KIWIS

MAKES ABOUT 8 SERVINGS
(It's hard to say what a serving is because normally you'll be mixing these with other things like granola)

Strawberries and kiwis are two of my favorite dried treats that are commercially hard to come by but simple to make with a dehydrator. Plus, strawberry-kiwi was a breakthrough Snapple flavor when I was in high school, so the big nostalgia points are there, too. You can make these to use separately (kiwi in the tropical snack mix, strawberries with granola or yogurt) or you can eat them together as a tutti-frutti, almost candy-like trail snack.

INGREDIENTS

2 pints (680g) fresh strawberries

3–4 fresh kiwis

1–2 tablespoons (13–26 g) granulated sugar (optional)

SPECIAL EQUIPMENT

Food dehydrator

MAKE IT

1. Wash the strawberries well. Hull them and slice them into slices ¼ inch (6 mm) thick. Peel the kiwis with a vegetable peeler or small, sharp knife and slice them into pieces ¼ inch (6 mm) thick.

2. Arrange the fruit slices on the trays of your dehydrator, leaving a bit of space between all pieces to allow the air to circulate. Sprinkle evenly with sugar. (This step is optional, but since both of these fruits are on the tart side when dried, I like it.)

3. Dry at 135°F (57°C) until they are dried through—if you tear a slice in half, there should be no signs of moisture coming out when you squeeze. Transfer the dried fruit to an airtight container. It is a good idea to keep the fruit in the container on the counter for about a week to watch it for any signs of moisture beading out or condensation in the container. If you do see this, pop it back into the dehydrator to fully dry.

4. Store in an airtight container in a cool, dark place until ready to use or pack.

MAPLE-BLUEBERRY FRUIT LEATHER

MAKES ABOUT 18 PIECES

Okay, first things first: Raspberry is the best flavor of fruit leather. The end. Honestly raspberry is my favorite fruit and so I like anything with raspberry. But I decided it was also too obvious, so I am giving you another favorite fruit leather. This one actually originated from the remnants of the cocktail syrup for the Blueberry-Maple Bourbon cocktail in my *Camp Cocktails* book! The blueberry-maple combination was so enticing, we decided to make it into a fruit leather as well. It is chewy and snackable with a flavor reminiscent of blueberry pie filling.

INGREDIENTS

4 cups (580 g) fresh or frozen and defrosted blueberries

¼ cup (80 g) pure maple syrup

1 tablespoon (15 ml) lemon juice

1 teaspoon vanilla extract

SPECIAL EQUIPMENT

Blender

Food dehydrator

MAKE IT

1. Combine the blueberries, maple syrup, lemon juice, and vanilla extract in a blender and blend until smooth.

2. If you want particularly smooth fruit leather, more like what you would get commercially, you can strain the fruit purée through a fine mesh strainer to remove any chunks. I do this for fruits and berries with seeds like raspberries, strawberries, or kiwi, but not usually for something like blueberries.

3. Line your dehydrator trays with parchment paper or the silicone baking mats they make for dehydrators, then spread the fruit mixture into the trays. Spread each layer out evenly about ⅛ inch (3 mm) thick with a spatula, making the edges a little thicker than the rest. This is a tip I learned to help ensure full drying.

4. Set your dehydrator to 135°F (57°C) and dehydrate your fruit leather until it is, well, leathery. How else am I supposed to describe it? It should take about 6 to 8 hours, but times may vary. It should be pliable and nonsticky to the touch. When they are done, allow them to cool fully before taking them off the trays. Slice the fruit leathers into your desired sizes of rectangle and roll each up with parchment paper. Store in an airtight container in a cool, dark place for up to 2 weeks.

MIXED DEHYDRATED VEGGIES

MAKES ¼-½ CUP (30-80 G)

Making mixed dehydrated vegetables is a great way to preserve their flavors and nutrients. Focus on any vegetables you want to use in your meals, be they tomatoes, spinach, broccoli, squash—you name it. You can make a single type of dehydrated veggie at a time or you can do a couple, as long as you make sure they are very thinly sliced and you check them as they dry, because veggies dehydrate at different rates. This is a simple recipe for dehydrating a mix of carrots, peas, zucchini, and corn (a.k.a. one of my favorite soup mélanges). But you can use this method for other vegetables as well.

INGREDIENTS

1–2 medium carrots

¼ cup (38 g) peas

1 small zucchini

1 cob of corn

Salt (optional)

SPECIAL EQUIPMENT

Food dehydrator

MAKE IT

1. To prepare vegetables, peel and slice the carrots into thin rounds, about ⅛ inch (3 mm) thick. Shell the peas if they're fresh or defrost if they are frozen. Slice the zucchini into rounds about ⅛ inch (3 mm) thick. Cut the corn kernels from the cob (alternatively use ¼ cup frozen corn, defrosted).

2. If desired, you can blanch the vegetables to help preserve flavor, but this is optional with these particular vegetables since they are all quite tender. With vegetables that you would normally want cooked, such as potatoes, broccoli, kale, or cauliflower, blanching is definitely preferred. To blanch veggies, bring a pot of water to a boil and prepare a bowl of ice water. Add each vegetable to the boiling water separately for a brief time, about 1 minute, or until the color brightens. Then immediately transfer them to the ice water to stop the cooking process. Drain the excess water, and dry the veggies on towels or paper towels before dehydrating.

3. You can sprinkle a small amount of salt on the vegetables for added flavor if you want your vegetables preseasoned. Make sure to account for this in any recipe you use them in.

4. Put mesh liners on your dehydrator trays so the little vegetables won't fall through. Evenly spread the vegetables on the dehydrator trays, making sure they are not overlapping. This ensures good air circulation and even drying.

(continued)

5. Follow the dehydrator's instructions for vegetable dehydration temperatures. Typically, vegetables are dried at around 125°F to 135°F (52°C to 57°C). Dehydrate the vegetables, checking them periodically, until they are completely dry and have a leathery or brittle texture. This can take anywhere from 6 to 12 hours, depending on the thickness of the slices and the specific dehydrator model.

6. Allow the dehydrated veggies to cool completely before storing. It's a good idea to store your dehydrated food in an airtight container on the counter for a week, watching for any signs of moisture or mold to make sure they are truly dry. If moisture appears in the container, pop the veggies back in the dehydrator for more drying time.

7. Finally, store the dehydrated vegetables in airtight containers or vacuum-sealed bags in a cool, dark place until ready to pack for a trip.

ACKNOWLEDGMENTS

A book only ever comes together because of massive amounts of work that go on quietly behind the scenes. A huge thank-you to Thom, Liz, Marissa, and the whole team at Quarto for keeping things on track, bringing all the details together, and taking timeline changes in stride while I did ridiculous things like break my right wrist playing hockey, making it impossible to cook or write. Thank you to Hanna for making gorgeous photos that capture the spirit of gathering and working brilliantly even when it had to be at a distance. Thank you to my wonderful family, especially Joel, Espen, and Vidar, for eating my food and putting up with me writing and testing recipes at all the most inopportune moments on vacation and in the middle of the night. I love you all more than you can know! And most of all, thank you to our dear friends, Sarah, Cal, Gigi, Annie, Janaki, Truman, Ellis, and our remarkable Bridge Club peeps. I wouldn't have gotten through COVID-19, and I wouldn't be getting through now, without you all.

ABOUT THE AUTHOR

Emily Vikre is a native Duluthian who holds a PhD in food policy and behavioral theory from Tufts University. She is co-founder and co-owner of Vikre Distillery, which was named Best Craft Spirits Distillery by *USA Today* in 2016. They have also won a slew of technical awards: a gold and five silvers at the San Francisco World Spirits Competition; gold, silver, and bronze awards from the American Craft Distillers Association; silvers and bronze from the American Distilling Institute; and two Good Food awards in 2018. A nationally recognized food and drinks writer, Emily is the author of *Camp Cocktails* and *The Family Camp Cookbook*. She was formerly a regular columnist for *Food52* and has written for *Lucky Peach*, Minnesota Public Radio, and *Norwegian American Weekly*.

INDEX